# Greenwich Council
## Library & Information Service

IN HOUSE QUALITY SYSTEM!

KT-178-511

**Eltham Centre Library**
**Archery Road, SE9 1HA**
**020 8921 3452**

---

Please return by the last date shown

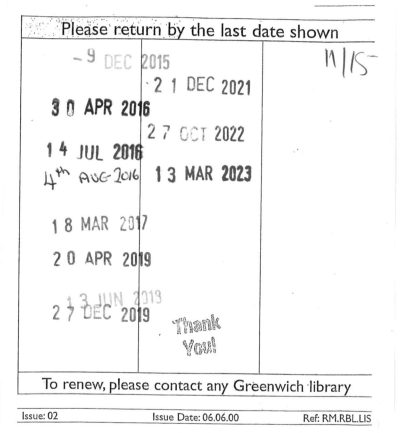

- 9 DEC 2015

·2 1 DEC 2021

3 0 APR 2016

2 7 OCT 2022

1 4 JUL 2016

4th AUG 2016    1 3 MAR 2023

1 8 MAR 2017

2 0 APR 2019

1 3 JUN 2019
2 7 DEC 2019

11/15

Thank You!

---

To renew, please contact any Greenwich library

---

| Issue: 02 | Issue Date: 06.06.00 | Ref: RM.RBL.LIS |
|-----------|---------------------|------------------|

# JOB

# How to Get That Job

The complete guide to getting hired

4th Edition

Malcolm Hornby

**PEARSON**

Harlow, England • London • New York • Boston • San Francisco • Toronto • Sydney
Auckland • Singapore • Hong Kong • Tokyo • Seoul • Taipei • New Delhi
Cape Town • São Paulo • Mexico City • Madrid • Amsterdam • Munich • Paris • Milan

**PEARSON EDUCATION LIMITED**

Edinburgh Gate
Harlow CM20 2JE
Tel: +44 (0)1279 623623
Fax: +44 (0)1279 431059
Website: www.pearson.com/uk

First published as *I Can Do That!* by Delta Management 1993
Second edition 1994
First published as *36 Steps to the Job You Want* by Pearson Education in 1997
Second edition published as *3 Easy Steps to the Job You Want* 2000
Third edition published as *Get That Job!* 2005
**Fourth edition published in Great Britain in 2012** (print and electronic)

© Delta Management 1993 (print)
© Longman Group 1994 (print)
© Pearson Education Limited 1997, 2005 (print)
© Pearson Education Limited 2012 (print and electronic)

ISBN: 978-0-273-77212-5 (print)
      978-0-273-72213-2 (PDF)
      978-0-273-77215-6 (ePub)

*British Library Cataloguing-in-Publication Data*
A catalogue record for this book is available from the British Library

*Library of Congress Cataloging-in-Publication Data*
A catalog record for the print edition is available from the Library of Congress

10 9 8 7 6 5 4 3 2 1
16 15 14 13 12

Print edition typeset in 10/14 Plantin by 30
Printed in Great Britain by Henry Ling Ltd., at the Dorset Press, Dorchester, Dorset

NOTE THAT ANY PAGE CROSS REFERENCES REFER TO THE PRINT EDITION

*Find a job you love and you will never have to work a day in your life.*

**Confucius, 5th century** BC

*I don't think of work as work and play as play. It's all living. I'm living and learning every day … it's like being at a university, studying a course you're really fascinated by. And in between all that, I am surrounded by family and friends.*

**Richard Branson, 21st century** AD

# Contents

# About the author

**Malcolm Hornby** Chartered FCIPD FCMI

Malcolm is a writer and business and personal coach. As a highly-experienced consultant and HR professional, he has an in-depth knowledge of career management.

In *How to Get That Job* Malcolm has combined his own life experiences and philosophy with his expertise in Human Resources and the job market. His positive 'can-do' attitude and pragmatic approach is summarised in the title of his first book *I Can Do That!* which he self-published, and on which *How to Get That Job* is based. Over two decades and several editions his books have helped many thousands of people through the career management minefield and have shown them 'how to get that job'.

# Introduction to the fourth edition

## How this book can help

There's probably never been a time when it's been as easy to *find* a job as it is today. But there can be few times in history when it's been as difficult as it is to *get* a job. The internet and new technology have given us instant access to all kinds of information, including job vacancies. At the same time the recession has hit us all, with companies going bankrupt and others making people redundant, or freezing their recruitment. *But* there is some light at the end of the tunnel: employers are constantly saying that they have skills shortages and how they have difficulties in recruiting the right staff. My recent trawl of the internet job boards revealed almost half-a-million jobs being advertised.

*How To Get That Job* will help you to search out the opportunities that are right for you and will get you the job you want. Since the first edition of this book was published two decades ago, it has helped thousands of people to find a new career direction, and to get a new job. Now it's your turn! I'll help you to identify what makes you special as an employee, to set your own goals and will show you the tips and techniques that will help you to get the job you want. There's advice on everything you need to succeed, from practical tips on how to write a CV to letters of application. Plus, you'll learn how to access the unadvertised job market, use positive body language, use the internet, give a great presentation, win in an assessment centre ... and much, much more!

## Does it work? Will it be worth it?

YES! And, YES! The techniques in this book do work and *can* help you to get that job. It gives me a tremendous buzz when I get phone calls and e-mails from people who have used the techniques to land a job. Like Peter, a manager who had been unemployed for a year. Peter had applied for hundreds of jobs without success. After using one technique from *How to Get That Job* he landed a job within a week! Or Heather, a school leaver, who followed the advice in *How to Get That Job* and got the first job she applied for, as a trainee veterinary nurse. John had been unhappy in his job in management for over a decade. He was 'liberated' by redundancy and used the techniques from *How to Get That Job* to get a post as a college lecturer.

## Ten life-changing ideas to bring you success in your job hunt

In my experience, most successful job hunters and career changers have a real vision of what success means to them and have a plan of how they will achieve it. I want to encourage you to 'take the initiative' for your life and your career. Before you start to read the chapters in *How to Get That Job* I'd like to share ten life-changing ideas with you. These ideas will help you develop a greater awareness of what you need and want out of life, so that your career fits into the life you want, rather than the other way round.

These tips will help you to 'raise your head high', improve your confidence and boost your chances of success in your job hunt by helping you to look at your long-term goals.

### Life-changing idea 1: we are all mortal – *Carpe diem*

Forgive me for stating the obvious, but none of us is immortal. Have you ever stopped to consider that once a day has passed, you will never have the opportunity to live it again? If you want a wake-up call for how many days you have left, try this little exercise.

Draw a horizontal line on a piece of paper. At the left end of the line write a zero and also the year you were born. Now try to guess/ estimate how old you will be when you die and write this number and the year at the right end of the line. Now draw a cross on the line to correspond with your age now. How do you feel about the time that has passed? How do you feel about the days and years to come? If, like me, you believe that you are in control of your life and you want to make the most of it, then read on.

## Life-changing idea 2: define *your* vision of success

When I was in my twenties I once became very disgruntled when a colleague was promoted ahead of me. 'Don't nail your colours to someone else's mast', advised my boss Alan. 'Don't try to live someone else's life.' That advice helped me to define my own vision of success and has stayed with me for the whole of my life.

Now I'm not saying that it's wrong to be inspired by people whom we admire. But we shouldn't try to copy their lives, or live a life that is dictated by the desires of others. What does success mean to you? What was your knee-jerk reaction to that question? A big salary increase? A promotion? A fast car? Seriously, when did you last sit down and write your definition of 'a successful life'? Have you ever done it? You see, I believe there are as many definitions as there are people reading this book.

So what are *your* criteria for a successful life? What is *your* life-vision? Remember, a vision is a dream taken seriously. Write down the words that come into your head and develop *your* definition of success. And the definition doesn't have to be driven by money. The 15 months that I spent working as a volunteer teacher with the charity Voluntary Services Overseas in Papua New Guinea count as one of the most successful chapters in my life, in spite of the fact that I was paid only a subsistence-level income.

> a vision is a dream taken seriously

## Life-changing idea 3: write a plan – develop your strategy

So now you know what success means to you, how do you get there? Writing a strategic life plan with set life goals will help you to achieve success.

So let me ask you. *Where do you want to get to in your life? What do you want to achieve? What is YOUR life plan?* I have asked these question of hundreds of people and been shocked by their answers. I've got used to it over the years: glazed eyes, dropped jaws and blank expressions. Doh! You'd think I'd asked them to give me the formula for some highly complex chemical, when all I'd really asked was '*What do you want to do with the rest of your life?*'.

The planning techniques below are also useful tools that you can use to develop ideas for your plan. As a starting point, write down 5–10 'life goals' for the next five-year period. These are the actions that can turn your vision into reality. You don't need to use all of the planning and analysis techniques, and different people prefer to use different tools. Whichever ones you use, you'll find that self-analysis will improve your self-awareness and this will help you to sell yourself better, whether it's in your job applications or interviews.

### 7 planning techniques

1   Mind maps. Write the word 'Success' in the middle of a bubble in the centre of a large piece of paper. Now let your mind free-wheel with all the ideas that can make it a reality. Read books by Tony Buzan for more.

2   Life pies. Analyse your life over a period of time – say a week. Log how much time you spend doing various things: working, travelling to work, socialising, playing with your children, etc. Use a pie chart to represent this. Then draw your 'ideal' life pie. Visit **www.eoslifework.co.uk/ getalife.xls** for a Microsoft Excel tool to help you do this.

3  Force field. On the right side of a piece of paper list everything negative that's holding you back. On the left side list all the positives that can take your life forward.

4  SWOT analysis. Analyse your strengths, weaknesses, opportunities and threats.

5  Goal setting. List all the things you would like to achieve in your life.

6  Personality profiling/self-analysis. Take on-line tests to gain greater personal insight; **www.keirsey.com** is a good starting point.

7  Obituary. Write your own obituary as it stands now! Then write it for ten years from now. How do the two differ?

## Life-changing idea 4: develop a PMA (positive mental attitude)

People often have problems in making career plans and developing goals because they impose barriers on themselves. They say things like 'I could never achieve this', 'That opportunity is not available to me', 'This isn't feasible', etc. How many times have you heard (or asked!) the question 'Is the glass half-full or half-empty?' and felt good about the positive 'Half-full' answer that you've given? Well, I'd like you to take your thoughts to a new level. Because unless you live your life in a vacuum, the glass is *always* full. Sometimes water, sometimes air, sometimes both, sometimes poison, sometimes nectar. 'The glass' is in your hands. The responsibility for making the most of the contents is, to a very large extent, yours. If you adopt the mind-set that you *can* make the most of what you've got, then you're halfway to success. Many successful sports people develop mental pictures of themselves crossing the winning line first, or scoring that winning goal.

In Susan Jeffers' inspirational book *Feel the Fear and Do It Anyway*, Susan treats every new life experience as a positive learning opportunity. Even when she contracted breast cancer, she adopted the positive attitude that it gave her a deeper insight into herself. It also gave her the opportunity to meet people whom she had never met before.

You can develop your positive mental attitude by reading inspirational writings, such as Kipling's poem *If* or any of the American *Chicken Soup* books. Watch inspirational films such as *Top Gun* or *An Officer and a Gentleman* or *Working Girl*, which show people's commitment to success. Convince yourself that you are in charge of your own destiny. Believe that you can achieve the success you want, picture yourself achieving it, and you're halfway there!

> you are in charge of your own destiny

## Life-changing idea 5: conquer rejection and fear of failure

Embarking on a job-hunting programme can be challenging, enjoyable and rewarding, but job hunting can also be very depressing because there is often a huge amount of rejection. When looking for new opportunities, your job hunt can often look like this:

| | | | | | | | | | | |
|---|---|---|---|---|---|---|---|---|---|---|
| no | no | no | no | no | no | no | no | no | no | |
| no | no | no | no | no | no | no | no | no | no | |
| no | no | no | no | no | no | no | no | no | no | |
| no | no | no | no | no | no | no | no | no | no | |
| no | no | no | no | no | no | no | no | no | no | |
| no | no | no | no | no | no | no | no | no | no | YES |

But you *can* succeed in spite of failure – if you're persistent and persevere. If you don't believe me that you can still succeed after failure, then here are some 'failures' that were never going to make it: Coca-Cola, Ford, Gillette and Heinz! I understand they all went on to better things, but: Coca-Cola sold only 400 bottles in its first year in business. Henry Ford went bust twice before his business successes. In its first year of trading Gillette sold only 51 safety razors and 168 blades! H.J. Heinz (of beanz fame) went bankrupt, learned the lessons and did better next time.

Two of the outstanding successes of recent times were one-time failures. Would you believe that Bill Gates' first business venture failed to take off: 'Traf-O-Data', a computerised system for processing paper tapes from traffic counters? In 2012 Bill Gates was listed as the second richest person in the world, with a fortune of $61 billion. And J.K. Rowling's story should be an inspiration to all of us as it truly epitomises the reality of a 'rags to riches' life story that can be achieved through perseverance and determination. In the early 1990s she was nearly penniless, severely depressed, divorced and raising a child on her own while attending university and writing a novel. She progressed from living on social security payments to being a dollar billionaire and one of the richest women in the world in a span of only a few years. In October 2010 J.K. Rowling was named 'Most Influential Woman in Britain' by leading magazine editors.

When I wrote my first book I was rejected by over 30 publishers. Undeterred I self-published. When I re-submitted the self-published version I got a publishing contract within 24 hours! Don't be afraid of failure. Treat it as a learning opportunity. You may have to 'kiss a lot of frogs before you find your prince'. But if you persevere you *can* succeed.

In my work with job hunters and my research for this and other books, I have found low self-esteem to be one of the biggest barriers to people achieving success in their job hunt, so I hope these stories of success will help to raise spirits and show that success can follow failure. For more inspiring stories of people who have overcome failure, ridicule and rejection and gone on to achieve success, see Appendix 2.

## Life-changing idea 6: prepare to change

Computer technology and the internet have given us a new way of doing business. You probably have more computing power in your mobile phone than existed in the entire world at the start of the 1960s. Technology has changed the way we work forever;

for example, the traditional role of 'secretary' has virtually disappeared from the workplace as managers take more responsibility for organising their time and creating their own communications using mobile technology.

Changes often mean the end of existing jobs and the creation of new work opportunities for people. Indeed, many organisations now value themselves in terms of their 'Human Capital'. *How to Get That Job* will help you to capitalise on your own 'Human Capital Assets' and take advantage of present and future job opportunities as 'traditional' jobs disappear and new ones emerge.

By the way, if you are sitting reading this thinking 'Well I'm over 50. I'm way too old for a major career change. Who's going to employ someone of my age?', or 'I wouldn't know where to begin thinking about creating my own job', or indeed any other negative thoughts about your continued success, then how's this for a reality check?

Ray Kroc was of Czechoslovakian descent and worked as an ambulance driver in the First World War. He subsequently moved to the USA and tried his hand at a number of jobs. By the early 1950s he was a Multimixer milkshake machine salesman. Two of his customers were the McDonald brothers, Dick and Mac, who were using eight of his machines at their innovative California hamburger restaurant. The brothers had recognised the potential of their business and had started to franchise it, but with minimal success. Kroc believed that the restaurant model had tremendous potential, and in 1955, at the age of 52, he acquired franchising rights to open a McDonald's restaurant of his own, in Des Plaines, Illinois.

*'I was 52 years old. I had diabetes and incipient arthritis. I had lost my gall bladder and most of my thyroid gland in earlier campaigns, but I was convinced that the best was ahead of me.'*

Ray Kroc

It was the McDonald brothers who invented the Speedee Service System, which established the principles of modern fast-food restaurants, but it was Ray Kroc who recognised the enormous potential. He encouraged the brothers to put him in charge of franchising, and founded the McDonald's Corporation with the opening of his first franchise.

Within six years Ray Kroc went from travelling salesman to successful businessman and, in 1961, he bought out the McDonald brothers for US $2.7 million. It is Ray Kroc who is credited in the history books as being the founder of the international brand McDonald's.

Ray Kroc died in 1984 at the age of 81 having built up a fortune of 500 million dollars in less than 30 years. His success is a lesson to all of us that life can begin at 50 if you have the passion and enthusiasm for what you want to achieve.

Job hunting is a personal change-management process. And of course we've all heard it said in the past that 'people don't like change' haven't we? Well, I'm sorry, I disagree. People *like* change! If people didn't like change then why do we look forward to going on holiday, buying new clothes, getting a new car?! People like change if it answers the WIFM question in a positive way: What's in it for me?

## Life-changing idea 7: re-invent and repackage yourself

As I said in idea 6, our working environments are continuing to change at a faster pace than ever and to succeed in your career you need to be adaptable and open to change. So what's your attitude to changing and adapting?

You may need to challenge your paradigm of your self-image and what you can achieve. In business, paradigm paralysis can cause missed opportunities. Inertia or fear sometimes stops people from challenging their personal paradigm. You have not been

genetically encoded to be a secretary, an accountant, a trainer
... you can take control and have the life that you want, but you
need to be brave. *'You cannot discover new lands, until you have the
courage to lose sight of the shore.'*

As you embark on your job hunt, keep an open mind about the
kinds of jobs you could do:

- listen to others with a totally different view (they probably
  have a different paradigm);

- listen to your own intuition and have faith in your own absurd
  ideas rather than suppressing them.

Paradigm shifts can create new opportunities. An excellent example of a successful paradigm shift is Lucozade. In the mid 20th
century Lucozade was a drink that helped people to recover after
a period of illness, but as people's health improved and health
care became better, the market for Lucozade became smaller and
smaller. In the 1980s Lucozade re-invented itself completely.
The manufacturers recognised the growing 'exercise' market and
repackaged the very same product as an energy drink for athletes
and sports people. If you want to get a measure of the success of
the 're-invention', just go to any supermarket!

What has Lucozade got to do with career and life planning? Well,
everything! Our working environments are changing faster than
ever. The rate of change continues to accelerate. A couple of decades ago, no one had heard of HTML, SQL, C++ or Java. Now
people who can speak these IT and website-assembly languages
can almost pick their salary! There is no 'one way' to plan your
career or to find a new job; the keys to maximising your potential
are flexibility, keeping an open mind and regarding change as an
opportunity not a threat.

## Life-changing idea 8: build and use your network

'*Ninety-nine per cent of advertising doesn't sell much of anything*', David Ogilvy (advertising guru). The success rate for networking is no better, and may be even worse! But when it does work, networking can bring powerful rewards and a new job! Just as the gardener reaps their rewards for working and fertilising the soil, you will gain rewards from your networking activities.

Networking is a proactive process of building and maximising relationships to help you to advance your career. Your network becomes increasingly important as you get older, or apply for more senior positions. Some people believe that as few as 25 per cent of jobs are ever advertised and that about 50 per cent of people over 40 find work through personal contacts. Some people network quite naturally, while for others the very thought of it makes them feel so uncomfortable that the hairs on the back of their neck stand up! Ironically, many people who are brilliant salespeople and marketers for their product or service draw a blank when it comes to self-marketing! The whole of Chapter 2 is dedicated to networking, and I would encourage you to build and use your network as soon as you possibly can in your job hunt.

## Life-changing idea 9: get a coach

'*There is no such thing as a 'self-made' man. We are made up of thousands of others. Everyone who has ever done a kind deed for us, or spoken one word of encouragement to us, has entered into the make-up of our character and of our thoughts, as well as our success.*'

George Matthew Adams

A coach will help you to turn your visions and dreams of a career/ life plan into reality. Do you know someone whom you can use as a sounding board for your ideas? As you develop your career and life plan, you will find it very beneficial to 'bounce' your ideas off someone else. Ideas can take on a new dimension when you explain them out loud, and inputs from another person can really help to motivate you into action.

A professional career coach may be a complete stranger who will take you through a series of exercises to help you formulate and refine your plans. Many coaches do this through an initial 1:1 meeting, followed by a series of telephone calls. Very few of us have the benefit of using a professional coach, but do not despair! What about someone who knows you well and whose opinion you value? What about a favourite uncle or aunt? An old school/college/university friend? A current or previous work colleague? A neighbour? A fellow member of a sports or social club? You will probably find it best not to use your partner. Please do not misunderstand me – I'm not advising you should exclude your partner from the career-planning process; not at all. But they may not be able to 'see the wood for the trees' because of their personal involvement.

THE BENEFITS: You will find that your plans are modified, refined and more *realistic*. And all it will cost you is a box of chocolates, a special thank you at Christmas or a couple of beers!

## Life-changing idea 10: DO IT NOW! *CARPE DIEM*

The first time I embarked on a major career and life-planning process I spent several hours over the space of a fortnight on it. I used the principles I have mentioned here, as well as many techniques that are normally associated with business planning. It was hard work but the investment paid off enormously.

It's easy to put things off and wait for the 'right time'. But the right time is now! Are you feeling inspired to get your job hunt under way? OK, switch off the TV tonight and start on your plan. Or, better still, do it now! *Carpe diem.*

the right time is now!

## Life-changing ideas recap

1 We are all mortal – *Carpe diem*

2 Define *your* vision of success

3 Write a plan – develop your strategy

4 Develop a PMA (positive mental attitude)

5 Conquer rejection and fear of failure

6 Prepare to change

7 Re-invent and repackage yourself

8 Build and use your network

9 Get a coach

10 DO IT NOW! *CARPE DIEM*

# Chapter 1

## How to find
## your new job

Since I wrote the first edition of this book, the internet has permeated many aspects of our lives. It's a playground, a shopping mall, the best library in the world and the quickest (and cheapest) way of obtaining and sending information that I know. E-commerce, the use of the internet in business, has well and truly come of age and it's still evolving. Very soon you will be able to drive to a new town and ask your tablet or smart phone something like 'Who needs a personnel manager in this area?'. And, hey presto, there will be a list of local vacancies! Whether we need it or not, it will soon be here.

For this reason, most of this chapter looks at the key ways of finding a job on the internet and then at the end of the chapter we will look at other ways, such as job fairs and recruitment agencies.

*'It is not necessary to use the internet if you are looking for a job. But not using it says three things about you. The first is that you have not yet grasped the importance of the internet as a tool for accessing information. Second, you are restricting your career plans to people and places you are already familiar with. Third, you are an ageing dinosaur crippled by technofear.'*

Tony Glover, writing in *MicroScope*, an IT journal

Ouch! That hurts, but he's right. You *can* get a job without using the internet, and many do, but using the internet in your job-hunt strategy will increase your chances of success. Some of the best sites have on-line communities, careers advice and career-planning resources so that you can conduct your job hunt from one site.

Imagine being able to go to bed at night, and when you go back to your desk the next day your own private army of researchers has scoured trade publications, newspapers and journals. They have also phoned a few thousand recruitment agencies and employers to find jobs that would be of interest to you. Sitting neatly on your desk is a small, but perfect, pile of 'ideal job' vacancies! Well, your dreams have come true. Don't ask me how it works, but all the recruitment sites have this facility.

When you register with them you can set up a process in which their computer will automatically search their database each day to see if any new jobs match your criteria. You then receive an e-mail to notify you of the new job!

Before we look at the ways to get the best out of the internet, let's look at some basic principles.

## Reactive and proactive job hunting

There are three kinds of job vacancies. Those that:

● already exist – someone has been promoted or left, etc.;

● are about to exist – as a result of retirement or someone moving on, or a company expansion;

● are created – because your approach convinces the employer that there is a problem to be solved.

There are two ways of job hunting:

● **Reactive** – you read the vacancies sections in newspapers, journals and the vacancy boards of the job centre. Estimates vary, but many believe that as few as 25 per cent of all job vacancies are ever advertised.

● **Proactive** – you combine your investigative and entrepreneurial skills to discover vacancies, and market yourself so that you get that job.

## Persistence and flexibility pay dividends

When I was a 19-year-old student, I borrowed the airfare to the United States and enough money to exist on for 11 weeks from my parents. (Students do get long holidays, don't they!) My travelling companion, Keith, and I arrived in Atlantic City, which is like Blackpool but around ten times bigger, in the middle of the holiday period. We had work permits and were sure that we'd be able to find jobs. We couldn't. American students start their summer holidays before the UK colleges. Every temporary job had gone. We spent three full days from 7.00 am until 10.00 pm calling at every hotel, restaurant, shop ... anywhere where we thought we could get work. We took a bus to Philadelphia and spent another day doing the same thing there. But no luck. We took a bus to Harrisburg. By mid-afternoon we had met a clerk at the employment offices who said there were no jobs in Harrisburg, but if we were interested in picking fruit he would take us that night to Gettysburg, where he knew there were jobs. At 7.00 am the next morning we waited for the bus to arrive to take us to the fruit farm. It didn't arrive. It had been cancelled. No jobs.

The Gettysburg address I had was 3,000 miles from home – we knew no one else and had just about enough money to survive for the rest of the trip! Back to knocking on doors. We also wrote a letter to the editor of the local newspaper saying how much we were enjoying our visit to the USA, but did anyone have any work?

In the meantime I managed to get a job – as a dishwasher at a Holiday Inn. Two days later our letter was published and a director of a shoe factory (who was English) rang to offer us jobs. Promotion! I resigned my job as a dishwasher and started at the shoe factory.

Two days after that, I received a call from a Howard Johnson restaurant asking if I wanted a job as a cook. I explained that I had a daytime job but was available during the evenings and at weekends. I started that evening.

I now had two jobs. A week later one of the other cooks resigned. I told the manager that Keith was available. He now had two jobs.

Persistence, flexibility, creativity and networking took the pair of us from being unemployed to having jobs that earned us enough money to repay our debts and finance our flights and an 11-week stay, which included a three-week, 11,000-mile tour of the USA!

Trawling the internet for jobs is an important part of job hunting but there are many other ways.

# Proactive job hunting

And there are two ways of proactive job hunting!

## Traditional techniques of proactive job hunting

- Identify potential employers and write to a named person – not the personnel manager (unless you're looking for a personnel job), but the person running the department.

- In addition to your internet research you can identify potential employers by taking a trip to your local library and doing some book research. There are literally dozens of directories. A quick phone call can confirm a name. When you know which geographical area and industry/public sector you are targeting, ask the librarian for advice on which directories will be most useful. Yes, of course there are on-line versions of all of this information, and if you Google each of the titles you'll find their websites, but unfortunately some have restricted access unless you pay a subscription. Some of the titles you will find useful are:

  *The Personnel Manager's Year Book*

  *Kompass: Register of British Industry and Commerce*

  *Who Owns Whom?* – a directory published by AP Information Services (see: **www.apinfo.co.uk**)

*Stock Exchange Official Year Book*

*Directory of British Associations*

*Kelly's Manufacturers and Merchants Directories* (regionalised)

Don't forget the Yellow Pages and other local directories. And also the membership lists of professional bodies, for example the Institute of Chartered Accountants in England and Wales, the Law Society, the Institute of Taxation, etc. There are also industry-specific directories. The list goes on and on – don't be put off. Ask for help and be prepared to do some digging!

- Write speculative letters and e-mails to headhunters and recruitment agencies. Build up your bank of names and addresses from friends and business contacts. Also, scan the newspapers and journals (current and previous editions) for people who work in your target area. An excellent source of names and addresses is the *CEPEC Recruitment Guide*.

- Contact the branch chairperson or secretary of your professional organisation.

- Network – first of all, brainstorm the names of as many friends, acquaintances and business contacts as you can. Telephone them and get to the point quickly. Have three objectives:

  1 To let them know that you're looking for work – so that they can keep their eyes and ears open.

  2 To ask them for the names of two of their contacts whom you might approach.

  3 To ask for their advice about opportunities/recruitment consultants/journals/ads they might have seen.

- Personal recommendation – if you have been made redundant, will your previous manager write to, or telephone, or e-mail people in their network to ask if they will meet you … Go on and ask!

## GOYA techniques of proactive job hunting

Get off your a***!

- Be prepared to put in a lot of effort. Job hunting should be approached as seriously as a full-time job, and it can be equally time-consuming. Whatever effort you have planned to put into job hunting, double it to a minimum of 20 hours per week and be prepared for a long journey. You need to put in some long hours. Be prepared to make dozens of phone calls and be prepared to write tens, or even hundreds, of applications.

> be prepared to put in a lot of effort

- Target small companies – with a few exceptions, the big companies are contracting while some of the smaller ones are growing. Also, in a smaller company you're far more likely to get to see the decision-maker. Go there in person.

- Do some internet research on employers in your area and draw up a list of organisations that could use your skills. Find out a bit about their products, services, etc. from their website. Now go to visit potential employers – arrive in reception, ask for the manager by name and be ready for a short interview. This is what salespeople call a speculative call – of course it doesn't work every time. In fact, to be realistic it won't work most of the time. But if you never do it, then it won't ever work. And you only need it to really work once, don't you? Be brave, try it! Remember what I said earlier about 'the glass is always full'!

- Set yourself a target to see five employers each week – either through formal interviews or through speculative calls as described above.

- Visit your old school, college or university, nursing school, etc. – students there may be aware of vacancies for people with the skills or knowledge you have, or they may be able to give you names to add to your network.

- Have lots of 'irons in the fire' – sometimes when people are job hunting they 'fall in love' with one vacancy. As the interview process proceeds, they exclude any activity in looking for alternatives. It's almost as if there would be some kind of disloyalty to this potential job. Even if you have a really strong prospect of a job, keep searching for and applying for others. If the 'hot prospect' falls through then you'll still have other options; or, better still, how nice would it be to have the option of picking between two job offers!

- Network in person – wherever possible meet people face-to-face, rather than on the telephone or by e-mailing each other. They may meet you for a quick lunch, a meeting in the pub after work, or for a coffee. They'll give you ten times as much information in a one-to-one meeting as they would in a telephone call or e-mail exchange.

- If you've been shortlisted for a job and are attending a series of interviews, put your heart and soul into it – but don't do it to the exclusion of all other activities. Keep job hunting.

- Be creative, brainstorm – try to think of novel and different techniques of finding out about new jobs. See if your friends can come up with different ways.

> think of novel and different techniques of finding out about new jobs

Can't be done, you may say? Don't close your mind! Someone once looked up my name and hand-delivered a nicely packaged box to the reception area of the company where I worked as a personnel manager. The package was endorsed 'perishable – urgent'. It was delivered to me immediately, straight into my office (not buried in an in-tray) and placed on my desk. The contents – two packs of sandwiches from Marks & Spencer, a can of fresh orange juice, a cream cake and even a napkin. A letter in the box, from a young woman, explained that she realised I was a busy person – perhaps if she bought me lunch then the time I had saved could be spent giving her a short interview? When she telephoned me two days later, I spoke to her personally and met her a few days later. She had jumped in front of literally dozens of people. Regrettably, we didn't have any suitable vacancies. If we had, she would have been near the front of the queue ... no, not because she bought lunch for me but because she was prepared to try something different! It nearly worked. What she did get were some contact names of people in my network.

PS: I'm not suggesting that you now start to feed every potential recruiter! I am simply trying to demonstrate that there are merits in thinking creatively.

Here's another example of determination reaping its rewards. It was given to me by a friend of mine who is a partner in a law firm.

*'When recruiting for a solicitor we used a headhunter, found an ideal candidate and he turned us down. Then I went to specialist agencies. Lots of CVs, interviews, etc. I turned down one person after interview as I was not convinced that she could develop the business enough. She wrote to me a couple of days later with her ideas for generating further business. I was impressed, had her back for a further interview and she got the job!'*

If you have an interesting job-hunt method that you have used and that has worked, write to me or e-mail me at the address given at the end of the book so that we can share it with your fellow job hunters.

You may be asking yourself 'Which job-hunting technique should I use?'. My advice is ALL OF THEM.

# How to use the internet in your job hunt

As I suggested at the start of the chapter, anyone in this day and age who wants to be taken seriously as a prospective employee *must* use the internet as part of their job hunt.

The recruitment process has changed so much that many organisations will now only accept electronic applications. I have even heard of managers receiving printed CVs and then requesting that the applicant submit the same information in electronic form. Many organisations, such as the Civil Service and a number of department stores, use on-line screening processes before they will accept an application from you. When you start to register your interest in a job, they take you through a number of on-line questions to screen you in or out of the process. These can vary from a few questions, such as 'Do you have a permit to work in this country?', through to full-blown personality and skills and aptitude evaluations.

Electronic information is fast and paperless, as well as being very economical. If the personnel officer receives an electronic application from a candidate this can be quickly and effortlessly forwarded to another person. Compare this with the old way of having to photocopy people's applications and then mailing them through the internal mail system.

Let's imagine that you live in Aberdeen and you want to apply for a job in a local factory. The personnel department is located at the head office of the company in Edinburgh. You send your electronic application to the head office in Edinburgh. The personnel department in Edinburgh quickly sifts your application to confirm that you're the kind of person they are looking for, and with the click of a mouse they forward your application to the recruiting manager in Aberdeen. A couple of years ago this process might have taken a week or more. Now it takes place in a few minutes.

The internet can help you enormously in your job hunt. Using e-mail will help you contact numerous prospective employers quickly and economically – just think of all the money you can save on stamps and stationery, and not having to buy newspapers or magazines! Using search engines and visiting recruitment websites and employers' websites will help you to unearth numerous employment opportunities. At the time that I was doing the research for this book, five of the country's top websites had well over half-a-million job vacancies between them!

> the internet can help you enormously in your job hunt

Using the internet is so quick and convenient; you can access the internet at any time of day or night. So you can carry out your job hunting in your own time and in the comfort of your own home, on a train, or more or less anywhere now if you have the right kind of technology. In some ways the internet can be too quick, and many employees, or should I say prospective employees, shoot themselves in the foot by their lack of attention to detail and by being impetuous in their rush to rattle off an application.

## How to find a job on the internet – recruitment websites

Recruitment advertising is big business and there's a lot of money involved. I don't know whether you've ever thought about what it costs to advertise a job, but here's an insight – the price for a full page in the national dailies can run into tens of thousands of pounds! And that's why there has been such an explosion of recruitment websites, or Job Boards as they are often called. Organisations such as Monster didn't exist before the advent of the internet. To fight back, magazines and newspapers now carry their recruitment advertising on paper and also on their websites, which is an added bonus if you're a job seeker as you can read the job adverts from the comfort of your home without the expense of buying the newspaper or magazine. There are thousands, if not hundreds of thousands, of internet recruitment websites, and it can be confusing knowing where to begin. Remember you're looking for a job – it's easy to be side-tracked into reading the local news or checking for this weekend's car boot sales!

You'll find links to all of these websites at my website: **www.get-that-job.co.uk**. You'll also find numerous other links to specific professions/industries.

### Recruitment websites

These are my top six recruitment websites, based on user-friendliness, useful information and number of jobs advertised.

## Six of the best recruitment websites

1  **Reed.** Claims to be the UK's top job site. They had 131,000 jobs advertised when I visited. That's a lot of jobs. **www.reed.co.uk**

2  **Totaljobs.** Were listing 98,000 jobs across the UK when I visited. **www.totaljobs.co.uk**

3  **Monster.** The UK website of the original Monster.com. **www.monster.co.uk**

4  **Jobsite.** Was listing 34,000 jobs. **www.jobsite.co.uk**

5  **Fish4jobs. www.fish4.co.uk**

6  The government's excellent website for JobcentrePlus lists a phenomenal number of vacancies. Search by location, industry, etc. **www.jobseekers.direct.gov.uk**

You'll also find other sources of help for job hunters in Appendix 1 (see pages 265–269).

If you go to Google and search the word 'jobs', again you'll come up with a list of numerous recruitment sites, but be wary of wasting time trawling the American sites – unless of course you're looking for a job in the USA!

Recruitment websites can help you in your job hunt in a number of ways:

- You can search for jobs by specific industries, job type or location.

- You can set up a job-hunt agent so that every time a job matching your search criteria becomes available, you get an e-mail.

- The websites carry a wealth of free advice.

- You can join communities and share tips with others.

- Most have a wealth of excellent job-hunting tips and other resources.

- You can 'post' your CV on the website – if you do this, remember to make a small change to your CV every weekend. Employers search for the 'freshest' CVs and if yours hasn't been refreshed for a while it will get overlooked.

- You can download their App onto your phone so that you can carry out your job hunt anytime and anywhere (almost!).

Aristotle said that you learn to play the flute by playing the flute, and you'll learn how to get the best out of recruitment websites by trawling their pages.

In addition to using the search facilities, I would recommend you upload your CV to all the top sites and also any that are specific to your industry or specialism. Make sure that your CV is as up-to-date as possible and that it is richly populated with keywords for your skills, experience and specialties. This is essential as it means that your CV will pop up when the bank of CVs is searched by recruiters and they will contact you to ask whether you are interested in applying for the job. Also, remember to keep refreshing the CV (see above).

You will find that some websites will be happy to accept your word-processed CV as it is; others, however, work to a standard format and use a menu-driven CV-builder to build your CV in their standard format. It can be a little tedious filling in all of the sections, and you won't be able to upload the CV until everything is correctly completed. Fortunately, provided you have spent time building a good CV, you won't need to re-invent the wheel and you can copy and paste most of the information.

## How to find a job on the internet – employer websites

Don't overlook employer websites in your search for a job. About three-quarters of employers post their vacancies on their own organisations' websites.

To find out names of employers in your area, Google 'Mytown Businesses'. You'll get numerous sites with directories of your local organisations, and with a little drilling-down you'll reach the vacancies pages of your local employers.

Employers' websites will often give you excellent careers advice on how to go about applying to them and will give you an idea of the kinds of jobs that are available. For an excellent example, have a look at the NHS recruitment website: www.nhscareers.nhs.uk.

## How to get help from special-interest sites

Professional associations and other specialised groups have valuable career-related information. These help to identify opportunities for different groups of our society, such as people with disabilities. There are sites for silver surfers, working mums and many more. Professional institutions have their own websites and these can be a valuable source of information. All of these sites can be excellent sources for information-gathering and networking.

Some self-assessment testing organisations offer their services on-line to help you evaluate your own skills, interests and values so that you can focus your career goals better.

SHL is a highly regarded producer of instruments that are used in the selection process. Go to the SHL website and click on the tab 'Practice Tests' under 'Resources': **www.shl.com/uk**.

Many university careers services have their own sites on-line. They are useful for career-related information, particularly for students, recent graduates, new job hunters and even career changers. You don't have to be a student at the university to access the information. As well as having links to job vacancies, they contain a wealth of information ranging from self-assessment tools to CV and interview preparation tips. Google 'university careers services'.

You'll also find other suggestions for sources of help in Appendix 1.

## Six of the best reasons why you should make the most of the internet

1 **It's free!** Once you're on-line you have access to a phenomenal amount of information, from thousands of free resources and help guides to job listings, as well as CV-writing tips, interview tips and other career planning tools.

2 **Search engines and keywords.** You can use keywords and search engines to find jobs from thousands of websites, literally within seconds.

3 **Go behind closed doors.** Most organisations have websites dedicated to vacancies and provide a direct link to their HR department.

4 **Networking.** The internet is the world's largest network, so it makes sense for you to network on the internet!

5 **Instant information.** The information on the internet is constantly being refreshed with up-to-date information, whether it's national or international news, or information on new jobs.

6 **Magical properties!** Well almost. We take the power of the internet so much for granted but it truly is a phenomenal tool. It has no geographical or time barriers and is available 24 hours a day, 365 days a year.

## Would you stand naked in the street?

Let me ask – would you stand naked in the centre of your local city, shouting to the world that you're looking for a new job and carrying a placard displaying your address, phone number, earnings, medical history, age and sex of your children, etc.? No, I didn't think you would! Watch out that you don't do the electronic equivalent on the internet. Internet-users reflect society, and while most people are honest and decent, some are not. Beware of what you tell to whom. While there are a number of professional bodies in the UK for people who work in recruitment, *there is no statutory regulatory body*. This means that, quite literally, anyone can register a recruitment website address and upload their website onto the internet in less than 24 hours. (It is illegal for them to advertise jobs that don't exist, however.) Do tread cautiously on the internet – once you have given out information, you can't get it back! Check out the credibility of internet recruiters and don't reveal personal details in chatrooms, communities and newsgroups.

## How to find a job through Jobcentre Plus

Because it is free to advertise a job through the Jobcentre, many employers and recruitment agencies place their vacancies with the Jobcentre before posting them on the internet or spending money on newspaper advertising.

Years ago the Jobcentre had an image of being only for low-paid or unemployed people, but things have changed enormously and you'll miss out if you do not include a visit to your local Jobcentre as part of your job-hunt strategy, and you do not have to be unemployed to visit the Jobcentre.

At the Jobcentre you can use Jobpoints, which are user-friendly touch-screens, to find information on around 400,000 vacancies held on the job bank. Jobpoints are as easy to use as a cashpoint machine and you do not need any special training or computer skills.

You can access the same information through the Jobcentre's website: **www.jobseekers.direct.gov.uk/**.

## How to find a job through recruitment agencies

Just as estate agents earn their fees when they sell a house, recruitment agencies earn their fees when they place a candidate in a job. So it's in the recruitment agencies' interests to have you on their books.

The kind of job you are looking for will determine which agencies you apply to; local, national, industry specialist, or executive search agencies specialise in senior level recruitment. A quick search of the website, newspaper or your professional journal will help you to identify which to apply to. Then a telephone call is a good idea; some agencies welcome speculative applications/ CVs so that they can add them to a database, while others prefer applications only for specific vacancies.

Register your CV with relevant agencies. Remember, they earn a fee if they are able to place you in a job, so just like an actor's theatrical agent they are effectively working on your behalf, even though their client pays their fee! If you are invited to interview by an agency, treat it every way as you would treat an interview with an employer. The employer has entrusted the recruitment agency with the job of doing the first sift, and if you don't make a good impression you'll be out of the race.

## How to find a job through job fairs

These are sometimes occupation-specific, such as IT, aimed at graduates, or focused on a particular town or city. Don't miss out on the opportunity to attend a job fair, even if they are recruiting people from a completely different specialism. For example, if you're a chef and there's a graduate recruitment fair in town, go along anyway.

Dress as you would if you were attending a job interview and make sure you've got an ample supply of CVs with you. Wander around the room to get a feel for who's recruiting and when you've identified your target organisations, visit their stands. As an introduction, ask the people who are manning the stand to tell you a little more about their organisation – let them do the talking first. Remember the employers attend recruitment fairs to 'sell' their organisation and to recruit talent. You could well find that you're in conversation with the HR manager, and just because the HR manager has come to recruit graduates doesn't mean that they have forgotten about the fact that they need to recruit a chef for the staff restaurant. The other alternative is to submit a written application along with the other 72 applicants, but here you are standing in front of the recruiter 'being interviewed'. Yes I know it's a long shot, but being tenacious and bold like this can pay off. Be prepared for a short interview; at recruitment fairs they often have little booths so that employers can do a quick pre-interview screen. If you're lucky, you might just get invited to a formal interview.

## How to set goals and organise your job hunt

'A vision is a dream taken seriously.' Put another way, from *South Pacific*, '*You've got to have a dream; if you don't have a dream, how you going to have a dream come true?*'

Goal setting can make the difference between success and failure in your job hunt and achieving your vision. Goal setting gives you targets to aim for. Organisations and businesses constantly use goal setting to help them to achieve things such as production and sales targets. Similarly, many successful people say that an element of their success is due to goal setting. Goals are specific – 'to be happy' is not a goal, it is an aim. Achieving goals is the process

goal setting can make the difference between success and failure

of putting one foot after the other, along the stepping stones that lead to happiness. A good test of a goal is to see if it is **SMART**:

- **Specific** – for example, if it is to get a job then list the title, type of organisation, etc.

- **Measurable** – what criteria will you use to measure your achievement?

- **Achievable** – you will become demotivated if you fail to achieve your goal – but don't make it too easy, make it challenging.

- **Relevant** – goals should relate to what you want to achieve directly.

- **Timed** – set a target completion date.

An example of a job hunter's goals could be: 'Each day next week I will make contact with a minimum of three people on my network list and will get two more names from each of them.'

A longer-term goal might be: 'Within four months I will get a job as a development engineer, in a medium/large electronics company, within 30 miles of home, on £X,000 per year.'

I know they sound a bit wordy, but 'I'm going to make some phone calls and I'm going to get a job in electronics' just aren't goals. Goals state what you need to *do* to reach your aims.

Goals can be short- or long-term and relate to all aspects of life. Use the following to help you to set your goals. Set the long-term goals first, then your short-term goals.

## JOB  My career and life goals

Personal contract: I am going to achieve the following career and life goals in the next five years:

| GOALS | Home and family | Work | Social and community | Self (leisure, study, etc.) |
|---|---|---|---|---|
| | 6 months | 6 months | 6 months | 6 months |
| Goal 1 | | | | |
| Goal 2 | | | | |
| Goal 3 | | | | |
| | 1 year | 1 year | 1 year | 1 year |
| Goal 1 | | | | |
| Goal 2 | | | | |
| | 2 years | 2 years | 2 years | 2 years |
| Goal 1 | | | | |
| Goal 2 | | | | |
| | 5 years | 5 years | 5 years | 5 years |
| Goal 1 | | | | |
| Goal 2 | | | | |

# How to organise yourself and manage your time

As I said earlier, job hunting is a job:

*job hunting is a job*

- Allocate some 'office space'. A PC/ laptop with an internet connection and a good printer are *essential*.
  You don't need the latest 'all singing and dancing' PC, you only need something fairly basic to surf the internet for jobs and for word-processing.

- Keep a diary or use the MS Outlook calendar and use it for both planning your time and for recording appointments.

- Ensure that you backup your files on a memory stick or other portable media.

- Work expands to fill the time available – set deadlines for each task.

- Set daily objectives – use a daily action planner or checklist.

- Prioritise the day's tasks: A = must; B = should; C = could. Move to the Bs when the As are finished, and then the Cs. Don't do the Cs first just because they can be done quickly.

- Block off times in your diary for different parts of your job hunt.

- Decide when you are at your best for doing things; for example, best at telephoning early morning, good at planning early evening.

**plan for tomorrow at the end of today**

- Plan for tomorrow at the end of today.

- Start each day by making progress against an A1 priority goal.

- After you have opened and sorted your mail/e-mails, handle each message only once – in other words only pick up a piece of paper or open an e-mail when you intend to do something with it.

- Gather non-essential reading together and scan it for 20 minutes each week.

- Add additional actions to your personal action plan as they arise throughout the day and prioritise them.

- Analyse your job hunt weekly to see how you are progressing against your goals.

- Do it now; don't procrastinate. This is particularly important if you are out of work and you have a vast abyss of time ahead of you. Force yourself to develop a sense of urgency to maintain momentum in your job hunt.

# Chapter 2

## How to make the most of your network

The benefits of
networking and
how to do it

A new word has entered the English language in the past couple of decades and has become increasingly important in helping people to get a job – 'networking' or contact development.

For many people it's something they have been doing for years quite naturally through personal contact or telephone calls, and more recently through e-mails and social media. For others (particularly people of older generations), the thought of it makes them feel so uncomfortable that the hairs on the back of their neck stand up.

You cannot ignore networking as part of your job hunt. In addition to the traditional methods of networking, using social and professional media websites such as Twitter, Facebook, LinkedIn and Plaxo will significantly increase your chances of success.

So what exactly is networking? Networking is the proactive process of maximising the relationships you already have and developing new contacts, and using these contacts to help you to identify work opportunities. Why is networking important? Some people believe that as few as 25 per cent of jobs are ever advertised.

networking is the proactive process of maximising the relationships you already have and developing new contacts

But someone must know about the rest! By widening your 'net' of contacts, you'll increase your chances of learning about these opportunities. Also, career consultants will tell you that networking becomes increasingly important as you get older. About 50 per cent of people over the age of 40 find a job through their network.

Networking is not about pestering people for a job to the point that none of your friends will ever speak to you. Neither is it about embarrassing people so that they feel morally obliged to help you, or even give you a job.

Networking is about approaching people genuinely to ask for advice and ideas on how you can get your next job – you aren't meeting them, telephoning or writing to them for a job. This is extremely important. When you make it quite clear that what you want from them is advice and ideas, you'll reduce their embarrassment about the contact and you will find them far more forthcoming.

On the practical front, just look at the power of numbers. Imagine you start off with the top 15 people in your network, you contact these and they each give you the names of two of their contacts. That's an extra 30 people and you now have a network of 45. You speak to each of the new contacts and get two more names. You now have a network of 105 people, and you contact your 60 new contacts and get two more names, now you're up to 225 ... hang on, let's not get silly! There will be people you can't contact for whatever reason. I simply want to show that, using this process, it's not difficult to have 40 or 50 (or more!) people helping you in your job hunt. People like to have their ego boosted by being asked for advice and I believe that most people will help if they are asked. You'll only embarrass them if it appears that you're asking them for a job.

Anyway, enough of their embarrassment! Some people find it very difficult to tell others that they are looking for work, so if you can overcome this barrier quickly you will be able to start networking straight away. So how are you going to say it? Look at the following expressions.

● **Words you might use to describe what happened in your organisation**

| Restructured | Gone bankrupt | We merged with another company |
|---|---|---|
| Contracted | Called in the receivers | We re-engineered |
| Downsized | The banks foreclosed | We had a change of management |
| Reorganised | We were taken over | We had a demerger |

● **Words you might use to describe what happened to you as a consequence**

| Fired | Organised out | Dismissed | Booted out |
|---|---|---|---|
| Sacked | Let go | Axed | Dropped |
| Given P45 | Said goodbye | Bounced | Let out |
| Made redundant | Surplus | Discharged | Terminated |

While one person might say *'You may have heard I got bounced last week when X went bust'*, another may say *'You may have heard that my company has been undergoing a downsizing operation due to the current economic climate. As a result they will be letting me go at the end of next month.'*

Think about how you will explain why you are 'back on the job market' to someone in your network. Bear in mind that words such as fired or sacked have a harsh bluntness about them (and can possibly leave people wondering if there was another reason), whereas expressions like 'organised out' and 'made redundant' are softer on the ear. In the lines below, write down why you are looking for work. Don't be self-effacing and don't be critical of your (previous) employer.

Now say it four or five times out loud.

The 'bottom line' is still the same, but you should now feel a lot more comfortable in explaining to people why you're looking for work and why you're asking for their help and advice.

## Who should I contact?

Many people think they have only a small network of personal contacts until they do this exercise. Go through your address book, e-mails, diary, business card file, customer records, correspondence files, etc. and brainstorm. Write down the names of people you know. Once completed, this list will be invaluable. At this point include anyone and everyone you can think of. Ask your partner and close friends for ideas. You have started networking!

### My Network

| | |
|---|---|
| Bankers | Competitors |
| Customers | Club members |
| Consultants | Doctor/dentist/solicitor |
| Neighbours | Professional contacts |
| Suppliers | University/college/school colleagues |
| Past employers | Relatives |
| Teachers | Work colleagues |
| Friends | Virtual friends |

Later in the chapter we'll look at how you can develop your network through 'virtual' contacts in internet chat rooms, social and professional media sites and forums. But for the moment we'll concentrate on using traditional methods.

## Now I've got my network, what next?

You need to identify whom you should contact first from your network. They will be:

- people you can contact relatively easily;

- people high in the organisation – the higher the better;

- people who could potentially employ you (even better);

- people on the same level as you, but with a different function, who can 'pass you on' to a peer. (Bear in mind that people on the same level as you with the same function may see you as a competitor. People on a lower level are rarely useful except for information gathering.)

Now choose the top 15 names on your list and contact them. Decide which approach will be best. As a general principle, the first choice is to see them in person, second to telephone, third is to write a letter and the least favoured option is to send an e-mail or text. Remember, your objective is not simply to inform people of the fact that you are looking for work, you want to motivate them to do something to help you. The more personal your contact, the more likely it is to succeed. Of course there are exceptions. If you're working in The Netherlands and have a friend in Japan who may be able to help you

> the more personal your contact, the more likely it is to succeed

to get a job in California then e-mail might work. But, then again, it might not! Don't get me wrong. I'm not a technophobe and I couldn't do my job as a consultant and author without e-mail. It's excellent for maintaining business contacts and exchanging information, but as a starting point for network development it's my least favourite option.

Whatever you do, get to the point quickly and don't waste their time. Achieve your three objectives:

1 **let them know you are looking for work** – so that they can keep their eyes and ears open

2 **ask them for the names of two of their contacts** whom you might approach

3 **ask for their advice** about opportunities/recruitment consultants/journals/ads they might have seen.

## How to use the telephone for network development

As I mentioned earlier, e-mails, social media, messaging and texts have their place in network development, but second only to a personal meeting for me is the use of the telephone. We communicate an enormous amount in the tone of our voice; on top of that, a telephone conversation is completely interactive!

To make the most of your networking telephone conversations, try using the following tips, which are given to telesales people:

- Make sure you have a pen and paper ready, along with any relevant documents.

- Smile – I know it feels silly when you're the only one in the room, but it adds sparkle to your voice.

- Stand up! All your internal viscera are pushing up against your diaphragm and squeezing the confidence out of your voice when you are sitting down. Standing up makes you more assertive and makes you sound more convincing!

- Have a clear objective of what you want to achieve, along with a fallback. For example, your primary objective may be to arrange an informal meeting; your secondary objective may be to call back tomorrow, when they have had a chance to read your résumé, to arrange a meeting.

- Make sure your language is convincing, fluent and understandable.

- Prepare your script in advance – write down your agenda/ checklist of what you want to say or ask.

- Practise your script – for example, the direct approach: *'Hello Mr/Ms―― I'm――. You recently received a copy of my résumé. I'm calling to see if we can make an appointment to meet informally to discuss any vacancies you might have for management accountants.'*

- Have your diary ready!

- Keep a written record of every conversation.

## How to overcome defences – using the telephone

The higher up the organisation you go, the higher and wider the barriers seem to become, with receptionists and secretaries seemingly having no other purpose than to protect their bosses!

The following techniques range from the polite to the devious. All of them work!

- Find out the secretary's name from the receptionist. Address him/her personally and repeat the name at least twice when requesting to be put through.

- When you're networking and you're put through to a secretary, say it's 'a personal call' (most managers will take 'personal calls' since most of them think it's a call from a headhunter!). Get to the point quickly. If it's a friend of a friend, make sure you clarify that straight away.

- Beat the system by calling the manager at around 8.00 am or after 6.00 pm (i.e. before or after work for most secretaries), or when the secretary is at lunch.

- If you try phoning most companies during normal working hours and ask for the name of the marketing director almost invariably the receptionist will tell you politely, but firmly, that they are not allowed to give out that information over the telephone. However, ring at around 8.30 pm and you're likely to speak to a lonely security guard, who is looking after the telephones along with the odd million-pounds-worth of building! Speak to them politely and explain that you want to call the marketing director the next day and you just wanted to make sure you'd got the right office. They'll be glad of someone to talk to and will probably reel off a list of names and extension numbers – if you ask for them, have your pen ready.

- Use a 'third-party recommendation', such as 'Mr Robinson, your personnel manager, has asked me to get in touch with …'

Remember, you may need to kiss a lot of frogs before you can find a prince! But persistence does pay!

you get one opportunity to make a first impression

You get one opportunity to make a first impression. The most powerful 'in' you can get is a personal introduction. As people give you names from their network, do what you can to make a positive first impression.

Don't overstretch yourself by using the blunderbuss technique. If you try to contact everyone in your network on day one you won't be able to handle the workload. Keep prioritising and manage the project – for example, follow up with a phone call if you've said you will.

Whenever you have made contact with one of your network, either in person or by telephone, send a short thank you letter or an e-mail. It costs little and shows your genuine appreciation.

# Keep working at it

Building a network doesn't happen in a day. Here are some great ideas for places and opportunities for building your network. They were kindly provided by Isobel Davies, an associate consultant and career coach with Macmillan International – and a member of my network!

## 20 ways to build your network

1 Mentor someone

2 Ask someone to mentor you

3 Get involved in task forces or other exercises

4 Send reports of your work to others who may be interested

5 Talk to others about what they are doing in areas that may be of interest

6 Look for development assignments or projects

7 Plan regular reviews to talk about your performance and your development with your boss

8 Prepare for your appraisal properly

9 Keep a personal record of your projects and accomplishments

10 Do a regular report on your and your team's exercises and send it to the people who might want to know

11 Offer to present at other people's meetings and bring others in to talk at yours

12 Attend training courses internally and externally

13 When you dig out useful information, think about who else it might be interesting to and forward it on

14 Attend conferences and seminars

15 Present at external events

16 Write papers and articles about your work for external publishing

17 Allow one evening a month for a drink after work with a friend or colleague whom you don't see often enough

18 Make time for the occasional supplier

19 Subscribe to networks that can contribute knowledge and information about relevant topics

20 Call one person a day whom you would like to talk to, but isn't on your priority list

## How to build your network using social media and other sites

A couple of weeks ago my 14-year-old niece told me that she had 1,200 friends on Facebook. I'm considerably older than she is and yet I don't have 120 friends, let alone 1,200. As you build your network using social media and other websites, do remember that the quality of your contacts is equally as important as the quantity.

The internet has really opened up a phenomenal new way of interacting with other people and building networks for mutual benefit, whether it be for finding out how to fix a car engine, travelling to exotic places or finding a job! As I have said earlier in this chapter, without doubt my favourite way of networking with other people is in person, with phone calls as a second best. That said, social media cannot be ignored as a method of building your network and taking you nearer to winning a job.

### Try this networking technique

Do you know anyone, anyone – a neighbour, a friend, a cousin, a friend of a friend – who works in an organisation that you're applying to? Save yourself the price of a stamp, and ask them if they would be kind enough to take your application into work and give it to the person who is recruiting. If someone is prepared to do this for you they are effectively giving you a referral, and your application could well end up way ahead of others.

You may also be doing them a big favour, as some organisations offer a bonus to members of staff who introduce friends in this way, as it can save them a lot of money in recruitment advertising costs. I know this technique works for a fact, as I once got a bonus of £300 for introducing a friend to the company that I was working for.

## How to use LinkedIn, Facebook, Twitter and others

### LinkedIn    www.linkedin.com

As a starting point, LinkedIn is a site that allows you to connect to people you know, but it is much more than that. It also allows you to see profiles of other people on LinkedIn, and enables you to connect to them. You can use LinkedIn in your job hunt and networking in a number of ways:

- Company search – making connections through connections. If you identify a company that you are interested in applying to, you can search on that company and hopefully find people who are connected to people in your network. You can then ask your contact to connect you.

- Employers post jobs on the site – the jobs are usually high quality, professional jobs.

- Communicate with contacts – you can let everyone in your LinkedIn network know that you are looking for a job through one single message, and as your circumstances change you can use the same process to update people.

- Slideshare – LinkedIn can connect directly to your Slideshare CV (see Chapter 4 for more ideas on how to do this).

- Blog and Twitter – your LinkedIn profile can connect directly to your blog and your twitter conversations.

## Twitter   www.twitter.com

Twitter is very different from LinkedIn as it allows you to connect with people whom you don't know, based on common interests. Because of this you can quickly make new connections and build your network. In addition, you'll see jobs advertised on Twitter that are not advertised anywhere else. If you were an employer, which would you rather do? Place a free posting on Twitter or pay thousands for a newspaper ad? You can search Twitter using Twellow: www.twellow.com. Just enter a company name or a person's name and Twellow will search the Twitter database of millions of members – and *growing!*

## Facebook   www.facebook.com

Facebook is primarily a social media site for connecting with friends or people you know or have known in the past, and because of this it can also be an effective networking tool for re-establishing contact with previous colleagues, etc. You can post notes and status updates on Facebook, either to keep your friends up to date with what's happening in your job hunt or to ask for help or advice.

In addition to LinkedIn, Facebook and Twitter there are literally hundreds, if not thousands, of networking and blogging and special interest sites, which you can use to build your network and advance your job hunt. These include **www.friendsreunited. com** and **www.plaxo.com**.

### Six of the best social media networking sites

1   **LinkedIn** An absolute *must* site for networking for professionals and others. Good for finding 'friends of friends' who work in organisations that you'd like to work for: **www.linkedin.com**

2   **Twitter** Great for building your network with people you don't know but have a common interest with: **www.twitter.com**

3 **Twellow** A powerful search tool that searches Twitter to find people and organisations: **www.twellow.com**

4 **Facebook** Great for connecting with friends or people you've known in the past: **www.facebook.com**

5 **Plaxo** Automatically updates your electronic address book and synchronises with your devices and apps: **www.plaxo.com**

6 **Friends Reunited** Another site that is great for re-connecting with people you have known in the past: **www.friendsreunited.com**

If you haven't already signed up to these sites, have a look at them and see what they can offer. Tread gently and only post information that you would feel comfortable a prospective employer seeing. Too many teens and twenties (and older!) have posted 'amusing' messages and images on Facebook and Twitter only to find that they have come back to bite them years later, when they have 'grown up'. It won't surprise you to learn that some employers Google candidates' names to see what else they can find out about them in addition to what they have put in their application. Some HR professionals abhor this practice and say that it's the technological equivalent of rifling through someone's underwear drawer, while others think it's fair game. The clip from the *Seattle Times*, below, gives you an idea of where this may be heading. I'm not going to comment on whether the interviewer was right or wrong to ask the question, only to say that employers are becoming increasingly thorough in 'checking-out' candidates, which means that candidates must do everything they can to ensure that any information about them puts them in the best light.

> employers are becoming increasingly thorough in 'checking-out' candidates

JOB    **Case study: Seattle Times – March 2012**

When Justin Bassett interviewed for a new job, he expected the usual questions about experience and references. So he was astonished when the interviewer asked for something else: his Facebook username and password.

Bassett, a New York City statistician, had just finished answering a few character questions when the interviewer turned to her computer to search for his Facebook page. But she couldn't see his private profile. She turned back and asked him to hand over his login information.

Bassett refused and withdrew his application, saying he didn't want to work for a company that would seek such personal information. But as the job market steadily improves, other job candidates are confronting the same question from prospective employers, and some of them cannot afford to say no.

In Chapter 9 we'll look at questions that interviewers can and can't ask, and how to handle them.

## Netiquette: seven top tips for social media networking etiquette

1 **Be professional.** Before posting anything, stop and think about whether the tone of the post is suitable.

2 **Be a giver, not just a taker.** Make positive contributions and help other people. Your good work will be rewarded by others doing the same for you.

3 **Listen to your followers.** Listen to your followers and interact with them. Social media is a two-way conversation, just like in the real world.

4 **Post relevant content.** The content you post on social media should always be relevant and interesting to your followers. It should also add value to the conversation you are participating in.

5 **Don't criticise others.** Your comments can be seen by a large number of people. Talking about someone in a negative way on-line will alienate people and give you a bad reputation.

6 **Be polite and respectful** to others and, in return, you will be treated with respect.

7 **If you have nothing to say, say nothing.** If you don't have anything nice to say, don't say anything at all. Don't post messages just for the sake of it.

Happy networking!

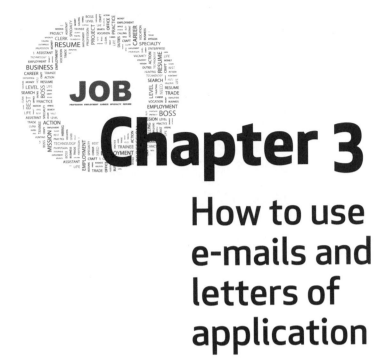

# Chapter 3

## How to use
## e-mails and
## letters of
## application

I f you can see someone in person, do it. If you can't see them personally, speak to them on the telephone. If you can't speak to them on the telephone, write a letter. If they are on the other side of the world, or you can only get their e-mail address, or you need a quick reply, send an e-mail. Both traditional 'snail mail' and e-mail have their uses and, realistically, you will have to write a lot of letters and send a lot of e-mails. Learn from the people in direct marketing who write letters to customers for a living. Why? Because through your letters you are trying to sell another person the idea that 'they should meet you', that 'they should look at your CV', etc. When it comes down to it, it's a sales letter.

AIDA is the copywriter's best friend. If you look at well-written 'direct mail' letters they follow the AIDA format:

A    Attention – the first paragraph quickly comes to the point to grab the reader's attention.

I    Interest – the second gives information to arouse the reader's interest.

D    Desire – the third paragraph describes the benefits you will gain and what it will be like for you to own the product or service.

A    Action – now that you want the product or service, what do you do? Telephone, fill in a form, etc.

Sounds simple doesn't it? Would that it were that straightforward!

As you write e-mails and letters of application, letters to networking contacts, letters to request application forms, covering messages to go with your CV, and letters or e-mails to recruitment consultants, make sure that you check to see if they follow the AIDA principles.

Try to see the letter or e-mail from the recipient's viewpoint. What impression would it make on you? What would you do if you received it?

## E-mail tips

I'm sitting in my office in rural Lincolnshire and have been catching up on some of my e-mails. I have just dropped notes on the desks of a client in San Francisco, a friend in Los Angeles, a friend who lives three miles away and sent a proposal to a client in London. The whole job took less time than it takes to go to the post box! The wonders of e-mail. I think I heard somewhere that it travels at 3,000 miles per second!

### Proofread until your eyes bleed!

When you have used your spelling and grammar checkers, print the document, re-read it out loud to yourself and then ask someone else to proofread and check your application. Julia Cardis, the author of *The Complete Idiot's Guide to Finding Your Dream Job Online*, uses the expression 'proofread until your eyes bleed'! Perhaps a little OTT and graphic, but it makes the point. So why all this fuss? Well, typos, spelling mistakes, sloppy grammar and poor presentation feature all too frequently in job applications. And what does the recruiter do? Delete and goodbye!

E-mail has revolutionised the way we work, and it varies from being the bane of people's lives to their most important working tool. I spoke to a number of recruiters when researching this text and was told that about 85 per cent of applications now arrive by e-mail, and that figure is rising.

The speed of information-exchange can be phenomenal. You can see a job advertised in the morning's newspaper, e-mail for information and have submitted your e-mail application, with completed application form and attached CV, before you have had your second cup of coffee of the day! I heard a story of a London-based firm posting a secretarial vacancy on one of the large recruitment websites at midday. By 2.00 pm they'd interviewed and appointed someone to start the next day. Clearly it doesn't always happen so quickly, but there's a lesson there for us all!

Correct use of e-mail is essential to your job hunt, so here are a few dos and don'ts.

| When using e-mail DO: | When using e-mail DON'T: |
| --- | --- |
| • Try to ensure that you make the key points of your message in the first screen-view. If the first part of your message doesn't grab the reader's attention, it's unlikely that they will scroll down. <br><br>• Understand the difference between urgent and important. <br><br>• Keep your message short. As a general principle, put your 'letter' of application in the body of your e-mail. However, if you have been asked to submit a letter of application then you should attach a well laid-out letter as a separate document, along with your CV or application form (tips on how to write your letter of application come later in this chapter). <br><br>• Put your telephone number and address at the end of your e-mail after your 'signature'. <br><br>• Print off any attachments before sending, to ensure that they are correctly formatted, especially if you have adjusted the margin settings on attachments. <br><br>• Check that the recipient can read your files if you are sending a letter or CV attachment. MS Word has become the 'standard' and I haven't yet had an occasion when someone couldn't read my MS Word files. | • 'Blast-mail'. I know it's easier and quicker to write one message and then group-send it to 20 or 30 recruiters, but put yourself in a recruiter's shoes. Which approach do you prefer, a personal approach or the blunderbuss? <br><br>• Use heavy shading or fancy formatting, or complicated graphics and photographs. Your message won't photocopy well and some companies use special filters to block large files and pictures, so that their information highways don't become congested. <br><br>• Send password-protected documents as attachments. Yes, it does happen. Your password protects your CV on your PC at work, so that colleagues can't read it. Then you see a job in the newspaper … Put yourself in the recruiter's shoes – you have had 60 applications for the same job. Are you really going to take the trouble to contact your mysterious candidate? Copy the information and paste it into a new file, print to check that it retains its formatting. Send the new file as an attachment and then delete! |

| When using e-mail DO: | When using e-mail DON'T: |
|---|---|
| • Ask for an acknowledgement of receipt; some companies block e-mails from free service providers, such as Hotmail, as a way of cutting down junk mail – so check that they have received your application. | • Use smileys and emoticons. |
| | • Delete your message once you have sent it. You'll want to refer to it if you get an interview. |
| • When writing e-mails you should adopt the same principles as when writing traditional letters. Ask yourself, 'What do I want the recipient to know and do when they have read my message?' | • Be over-familiar. Remember this is a business contact, not a bit of banter with an old school mate. |
| | • Keep re-sending messages in a two-way conversation. Delete all but the most recent message. |
| • Use an attention-grabbing subject line. | |
| • Use short sentences (35 words at most). | • Pressurise yourself into rushing and making mistakes just because you're communicating electronically; take your time. |
| • Use your spell checker and grammar checker. | |

## Speculative applications and approaches by e-mail

The same rules apply here – remember the AIDA formula.

There are many ways to find out someone's e-mail address, such as telephoning a receptionist or sending a message to their company's postmaster, for example postmaster@Get-That-Job.co.uk. Most company websites contain e-mail addresses, but these are often only general enquiries addresses. If you want to target your approach you may have to do some digging. There are a number of internet directory sites, such as **www.whowhere.com**, and many search engines such as Google, Yahoo! and Netscape that provide access to e-mail directories. Not surprisingly, the majority of sites cater for the USA, but the UK is catching up. One thing to bear in mind is that you might just find someone's personal or family e-mail address, and you might do more harm than good by sending an e-mail to them at home rather than work. Also, you'll need to be sure that you're sending your e-mail to the right Jane Doe!

The following pages contain some general tips on letter writing, which many people who are unused to letter writing find useful. Job applications by e-mail or letter are not the place for sloppy writing or informal chit-chat. You can also use the 'model letters' to help you in the wording of e-mails. Obviously you won't need to include things such as the address. The time and date of your message, as well as your e-mail address, will be shown to the recipient automatically, but the same levels of formality that you would use in a traditional letter should be used in e-mails.

## Letter-writing tips

Whilst most applications are done on-line nowadays, many employers still do ask for written letters of application and printed CVs.

● Use good-quality A4 paper, ideally 90 or 100 gsm. Matching envelopes create a good impression too. If you really want to push the boat out, get some stationery printed at your high-street print shop, although in this day and age you can produce almost as good an effect with your word processor. (Don't ask for the address to be printed in blue – it doesn't photocopy too well.)

● Unless you have been asked specifically to submit a handwritten application, your letter of application should be written using your word processor. If you're asked to send a hard copy, make sure your printer is set to the best print quality. Do not, under any circumstances, send a photocopied CV.

● There should be no spelling mistakes, grammatical errors or scruffy layout. But that surely can't happen! Don't you believe it! When I recruited a secretary recently, I rejected over half of the applications for these reasons. The advertisement asked for 'accuracy'! Fortunately, modern software packages check as you type. If it's an older package, make sure you run the spell check and the grammar check.

> there should be no spelling mistakes, grammatical errors or scruffy layout

● Write to a named person whenever you can.

- 'Dear Mr' is straightforward for men. If you don't know whether a woman is a 'Mrs' or 'Miss' then 'Ms' is the safest bet these days. These named letters end 'Yours sincerely' (small 's').

- When you have to write 'Dear Sir' or 'Dear Madam' (note, no 'e' at the end) then these letters end 'Yours faithfully' (small 'f').

- If an advertisement asks you to apply to Peter Butler do not start the letter 'Dear Peter' – it's over familiar unless you know Peter personally. Even then be cautious, since your letter may be photocopied and circulated to other people.

- Be succinct – get to the point quickly. If your letter is more than one page long, then edit it to fit on one page.

- Match the skills and knowledge that you have to those the recruiter is looking for, i.e. those mentioned either in the job description or the advertisement. We'll look at ways to do this in the next chapter.

- Never, never, never be self-effacing – 'I'm not quite what you're looking for but I'll give it a go anyway!' And don't point out anything that is missing from your portfolio of skills and knowledge. It's their job to spot that!

I know from speaking to job hunters that people can sometimes find themselves sitting staring at a blank screen or staring out of the window, looking for inspiration on how to word a letter.

On the following pages I have included some sample letters that I hope you'll be able to use as inspiration as you adapt them and make them your own.

**Warning!** One of the wonderful things about modern word-processing packages is that you can do mail merges, cut and paste information and copy files all with the click of a mouse and a few keystrokes. Check that the name at the start of the address matches the salutation (the Dear Mr or Ms bit). If you haven't got an eye for detail, ask someone who can proofread to check for you. Letters addressed to Colonel Mustard that start 'Dear Professor Plum' go straight into the bin! And take my word for it, it does happen.

## Letter to request an application form

> 4 Stable Cottages
> Abthorpe
> Northamptonshire
> NN12 8QT
> Tel 123 7777777
>
> 23 March 2012

Mr G. Choice
Moderate Corporation
Science Park
Daventry Road
Northants
NN99 99NN

Dear Mr Choice

### RE: CE/23393

I noticed your advertisement in the *Chronicle & Echo* newspaper for a laboratory supervisor. I would be very grateful if you will send me an application form.

I look forward to hearing from you.

Yours sincerely

Janet Dickson (Mrs)

## Note

● Don't enclose a CV or anything else at this point. Follow their system.

## Covering letter for a CV or application form

4 Stable Cottages
Abthorpe
Northamptonshire
NN12 8QT
Tel 123 7777777

23 March 2012

Mr G. Choice
Moderate Corporation
Science Park
Daventry Road
Northants
NN99 99NN

Dear Mr Choice

I would like to apply for the post of accounts supervisor that was advertised recently in the *Chronicle & Echo*.

I have read the job description with great interest and enclose my completed application form.

I look forward to hearing from you.

Yours sincerely

Janet Dickson (Mrs)

### Notes

- Don't antagonise them by implying that you're bound to get an interview. If you are too presumptuous you'll turn them off.

- This letter does very little, however, to help the recruiter to match the candidate to the job. It would have been a good idea to include three or four benefit statements (see Chapter 6, How to Sell Yourself).

## Response to an advertised vacancy

4 Stable Cottages
Abthorpe
Northamptonshire
NN12 8QT
Tel 123 7777777

23 March 2012

Mr G. Choice
Moderate Corporation
Science Park
Daventry Road
Northants
NN99 99NN

Dear Mr Choice

**Ref: MCC/737 – Production manager: Chronicle & Echo, 22nd May 2012**

I am writing in response to the above advertisement and wish to apply for the position.

You will see from my CV that, for the past five years, I have managed a plant manufacturing shampoos and hair colourants on a continuous production basis. Many of the production features appear to be very similar to your own. Previously I worked as Materials Planning Manager in a high-volume batch production plant.

I believe I have all the qualities you have outlined in your advertisement; I am ISO 9000 trained, a strong leader and have a capacity for hard work.

I am now seeking a position where my experience and expertise can be fully utilised.

I look forward to hearing from you.

Yours sincerely

Janet Dickson (Mrs)

## Note

● This letter highlights what the candidate has to offer against the recruiter's requirements, but isn't a 'rewrite' of the CV.

## A speculative letter to a targeted potential employer

4 Stable Cottages
Abthorpe
Northamptonshire
NN12 8QT
Tel 123 7777777

23 March 2012

Mr G. Choice
Moderate Corporation
Science Park
Daventry Road
Northants
NN99 99NN

Dear Mr Choice

**Ref: An Opportunity to Increase Your Market Share and Reduce Operating Costs**

As the Marketing Director (Electronic Products) of a £50m turnover UK Company, I have initiated and managed improvement programmes that have reversed sales and profit declines.

Some of my achievements include:
- launching six new products over the last two years and increasing market share substantially
- increasing sales by 12% by exploiting new markets
- reducing marketing operation overheads by £125,000 by introducing effective controls
- introducing networked computer-based information and financial control systems to improve customer response times and invoicing
- sales and profit forecasting on a monthly basis with 90%+ accuracy.

My CV is enclosed as I am now actively looking for a new position. I would be very glad to give you more information or to come and see you.

Yours sincerely

Janet Dickson (Mrs)

## Note

- Four or five achievement statements should be just right. You want to stimulate their interest and leave them wanting to know more.

# Making something out of nothing

> 4 Stable Cottages
> Abthorpe
> Northamptonshire
> NN12 8QT
> Tel 123 7777777
>
> 23 March 2012
>
> Mr G. Choice
> Moderate Corporation
> Science Park
> Daventry Road
> Northants
> NN99 99NN
>
> Dear Mr Choice
>
> It was kind of you to read my CV and write to me on 19th March.
>
> I was disappointed to learn that there are no openings in your company. It would have been a fortunate coincidence if my letter had reached you when you were recruiting for someone with my background.
>
> May I ask you whether you can suggest the names of any other people whom I might contact?
>
> I know that managers like yourself are often asked by others to 'keep their eyes open' for people with my skills and knowledge. I would very much appreciate you referring me to any of your acquaintances who might be interested. I will welcome any additional suggestions that you can give.
>
> Many thanks in anticipation.
>
> Yours sincerely
>
> Janet Dickson (Mrs)

## Note

- What have you got to lose? This letter is also worth trying with recruitment consultants – they may refer you to a 'competitor'.

## Speculative letter to a recruitment consultant

4 Stable Cottages
Abthorpe
Northamptonshire
NN12 8QT
Tel 123 7777777

23 March 2012

Ms H. Hunter
Choose Well Consultants
Northampton Road
Wappenham
Northants
NN99 9NN

Dear Ms Hunter

I am seeking a new appointment where my general management experience in the hotel and catering industry can be used. Any dynamic and developing business area that involves direct customer contact would particularly interest me. I am also keen to continue to develop my general management skills.

My present company is undergoing a period of substantial change and so I believe this is an ideal opportunity to review my career to date and investigate other possibilities.

I am willing to relocate within Europe. My current remuneration package includes a basic salary of £36,000 per annum, a 10% (variable) bonus, fully expensed car, private healthcare and a non-contributory pension scheme.

I enclose my CV and would be glad of any advice you can provide.

Yours sincerely

Janet Dickson (Mrs)

## Note

- Note that salary package details should be included in approaches to recruitment consultants so that they can match you against vacancies. Also, different consultants often deal with jobs at different levels.

# Follow-up thank you letter after networking

4 Stable Cottages
Abthorpe
Northamptonshire
NN12 8QT
Tel 123 7777777

23 March 2012

Mr G. Choice
Moderate Corporation
Science Park
Daventry Road
Northants
NN99 99NN

Dear Mr Choice

Many thanks for meeting me last week. I really did appreciate the comments you made about the way I have embarked on my job hunt.

Thank you also for putting me in contact with Simon and Pat. I have arranged to meet Pat next week, but Simon seems to spend all of his time in meetings – I'll keep trying!

I'll let you know how I get on.

Kind regards

Yours sincerely

Janet Dickson (Mrs)

## Note

- This letter is far less formal than any of the others, but is still businesslike.

- If you promise a friend that you'll let them know how you got on, then do it – they will want to know, and in a couple of weeks they may have some new information for you!

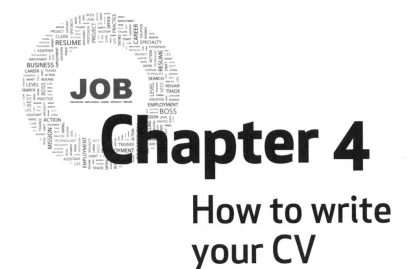

# Chapter 4

## How to write your CV

What to include, how to lay yours out

I magine yourself in your smartest clothes, looking as well groomed as you have ever looked in your life and carrying that facial expression of quiet (but not arrogant) confidence. Your CV (curriculum vitae) or résumé, or as some call it 'personal and career history', is a written equivalent of the mental picture you have just formed. In almost all the contacts you make, whether networking, speculative applications or responses to advertisements, your CV and introductory e-mail or letter will make the difference as to whether or not you get an interview.

The decision between a 'regret' (sorry you've missed your chance), a 'regret, but hold' (you're not exactly what we're looking for at present but we'll keep your details on file) and an 'invite for interview' can be made in as little as 30 seconds! I am being serious – that immaculately presented CV, beautifully written letter of application and the application form that took you two hours to write can be scanned by a recruiter and a decision made in less than a minute! Even worse, if it's an electronic application and it doesn't contain the correct keywords (more of these later), it may be scanned and rejected by a computer without ever being seen by a human!

If you think this is unrealistic then look at it from the recruiter's point of view and pity Geoff, a colleague of mine, who advertised two jobs in a car assembly plant and got 1,400 replies! If Geoff had spent just one minute looking at each application that would have taken 1,400 minutes, or a total of almost 24 hours non-stop! Beth, another friend, who is a personnel manager, was so overwhelmed with responses to an advertisement for a secretary that all applications in brown envelopes and all applications with second-class stamps were rejected. Two hundred responses to an advertisement is not at all uncommon. With applications on-line it can be even more, and you may find yourself competing with people from all parts of the globe. You see, recruitment is a (legal) positive discriminatory process! The recruiter is 'filtering out' all those people who don't match the selection criteria, and keeping those who do. When you apply to larger organisations, or through a recruitment agency or through a website, you may well find that your application is even scanned by software for word-matches – these are called 'keywords'. If the software doesn't find the criteria the recruiter is looking for, the software generates an automatic 'thank you but no thank you' e-mail … and maybe all because you typed ProductManager instead of Product Manager.

You need to help the recruiter positively to 'screen you in'. The job of your CV is to take you through the screening process to an interview. In this chapter we'll look at the essential steps you need to take to build a job-winning CV. In the earlier part of the chapter we'll look at the importance of gathering the correct information for writing your CV and we'll then have a look at the different kinds of CVs and how they are presented, whether on paper, electronically on-line or even as slide-shows or videos.

## ASK – the key to a job-winning CV

Attitude, Skills and Knowledge are your job-hunting currency. As we go through life, we develop our attitudes (personality and values), skills and knowledge, either wittingly or unwittingly. Not surprisingly, when employers recruit someone for a job they are looking for someone with the right mix of attitude, skills and knowledge. Having a good personal insight is essential to writing a winning CV, and so before we look at the essential elements of your CV we are going to carry out an audit to identify the qualities you have built up during your life, so that you can identify the transferable attitudes, skills and knowledge that you can take into your new job.

List below words that describe, in a positive way, your attitudes, skills and the knowledge that might be useful in your new job. You're probably thinking, 'There's far too much room!' Try it anyway.

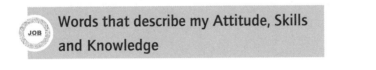

**Words that describe my Attitude, Skills and Knowledge**

What you have just listed is probably the tip of the iceberg. The best candidates are the ones with the best personal insight, who use this information to write a CV that sells so well that it wins an interview.

# Attitude audit

This first audit will give you a deeper understanding of your attitudes and personality and how you prefer to get along with other people. You don't need me to tell you that people come in all shapes, sizes and personalities! For example, some people are the life and soul of the party, dress flamboyantly and speak in loud, fast voices – get two of them together and it's almost a competition to see who can burst the other's eardrums! Other people like to conduct business in a very formal way, they're abrupt and to the point and are interested only in 'the bottom line'. It is often said that if you want to get along with others better, then the best starting point is to understand yourself.

The *Communication Style Inventory–SADI©* on the following pages, will help you to understand your own preferred communication style and give you an insight into elements of your 'attitude'.

Be honest and realistic when completing your answers. Do not complete the inventory as you think you *should* act, or as you would *like* to act, but how you believe you really *do* act in work situations. Give each question considered thought. There is no time limit and there are no trick questions. Once you have completed the inventory you will be able to analyse your results and read about your preferred communication style.

## 🔘 Communication Style Inventory–SADI©

**CSI–SADI** contains 28 pairs of statements, which relate to the way people behave in work situations. For each pair of statements, you have five points to distribute between the two alternatives (A and B). Base your answers on your knowledge of your behaviour. Your scores must be whole numbers – no fractions!

---

### How to score your answers. If . . .

| | |
|---|---|
| A is very characteristic of me and B is very uncharacteristic | A = 5 and B = 0 |
| A is fairly characteristic of me and B is fairly uncharacteristic | A = 4 and B = 1 |
| A is more characteristic of me than B | A = 3 and B = 2 |
| B is more characteristic of me than A | B = 3 and A = 2 |
| B is fairly characteristic of me and A is fairly uncharacteristic | B = 4 and A = 1 |
| B is very characteristic of me and A is very uncharacteristic | B = 5 and A = 0 |

**Remember, the numbers you assign to each pair of statements must add up to 5**

---

### Example

**When I think about my own decision-making style: A is fairly characteristic of me; B is fairly uncharacteristic. So I would mark my responses as follows:**

| 17A | 4 | am fast-paced in my decision making |
|---|---|---|
| 17B | 1 | take time to reach well thought-out decisions |

### When thinking about my behaviour with other people at work, I:

| 1A | ____ | prefer an informal and relaxed work environment |
|---|---|---|
| 1B | ____ | prefer a formal and businesslike work environment |
| 2A | ____ | am slow and deliberate in my actions |
| 2B | ____ | am fast and spontaneous in my actions |

3A  ____  am adaptable in my approach to people and situations

3B  ____  am predictable in my approach to people and situations

4A  ____  am disciplined and structured about the way other people use my time

4B  ____  am flexible about the way other people use my time

5A  ____  express my opinions freely in groups, without being asked

5B  ____  tend to contribute in groups when invited to do so

6A  ____  am usually willing to negotiate the outcome of situations

6B  ____  am usually reluctant to negotiate the outcome of situations

7A  ____  focus on the feelings and opinions of others during discussions

7B  ____  focus on the facts and business issues during discussions

8A  ____  respond to conflict situations slowly and indirectly

8B  ____  respond to conflict situations quickly and directly

9A  ____  am usually willing to change my opinions and ideas

9B  ____  am not usually willing to change my opinions and ideas

10A  ____  keep my personal feelings and thoughts private

10B  ____  discuss my feelings freely with others

11A  ____  take the initiative to introduce myself in social situations

11B  ____  tend to wait for others to introduce themselves to me in social situations

12A  ____  am flexible in my approach to dealing with people and situations

12B  ____  am predictable in my approach to dealing with people and situations

13A  ____  prefer to work in a group with others

13B  ____  prefer to work on my own

| | | |
|---|---|---|
| 14A | ___ | am cautious and predictable in my approach to risk and change |
| 14B | ___ | am dynamic and unpredictable in my approach to risk and change |
| 15A | ___ | quickly adapt to new systems and working practices |
| 15B | ___ | like to take my time to adapt to new systems and working practices |
| 16A | ___ | prefer to focus primarily on business ideas and results |
| 16B | ___ | prefer to focus primarily on people and their feelings |
| 17A | ___ | am fast-paced in my decision making |
| 17B | ___ | take time to reach well thought-out decisions |
| 18A | ___ | like to cope with many different situations at the same time |
| 18B | ___ | prefer to handle one thing at a time |
| 19A | ___ | tend to get to know many people personally |
| 19B | ___ | tend to get to know only a few people personally |
| 20A | ___ | tend to keep my opinions to myself, and prefer to offer them when asked |
| 20B | ___ | state my opinions freely without being asked |
| 21A | ___ | tend to make my decisions based on facts or evidence |
| 21B | ___ | tend to make my decisions based on feelings or opinions |
| 22A | ___ | like to actively seek out new experiences and situations |
| 22B | ___ | tend to choose known or familiar situations and relationships |
| 23A | ___ | am an intuitive decision maker |
| 23B | ___ | am a rational decision maker |
| 24A | ___ | am non-confrontational and comfortable with a slow pace |
| 24B | ___ | am direct with others and can be impatient when things move slowly |

| 25A | ____ | share my personal feelings and emotions in conversation |
|-----|------|----------------------------------------------------------|
| 25B | ____ | control my personal feelings and emotions in conversation |
| 26A | ____ | tend to dominate conversation in group discussions |
| 26B | ____ | tend to make infrequent well thought-out inputs in group discussions |
| 27A | ____ | am more interested in people's opinions than facts |
| 27B | ____ | am more interested in facts than people's opinions |
| 28A | ____ | tend to move at a controlled pace |
| 28B | ____ | tend to move at a fast pace |

C S I–SADI and the four circle model are copyright Delta-Management.co.uk Ltd.

When you have completed the inventory and **checked to make sure that the score for each pair of questions adds up to five,** transfer your scores to the table opposite. **Please take care when transferring your scores, as the A–B order changes in some of the rows.**

| E | R | S | L | SAH + (These are positive numbers) | SAL – (These are negative numbers) |
|---|---|---|---|---|---|
| 1A | 1B | 2B | 2A | 3A + | 3B – |
| 4B | 4A | 5A | 5B | 6A + | 6B – |
| 7A | 7B | 8B | 8A | 9A + | 9B – |
| 10B | 10A | 11A | 11B | 12A + | 12B – |
| 13A | 13B | 14B | 14A | 15A + | 15B – |
| 16B | 16A | 17A | 17B | 18A + | 18B – |
| 19A | 19B | 20B | 20A | | |
| 21B | 21A | 22A | 22B | | |
| 23A | 23B | 24B | 24A | | |
| 25A | 25B | 26A | 26B | | |
| 27A | 27B | 28B | 28A | | |
| E Total | R Total | S Total | L Total | SAH Total + | SAL Total – |

Compare your **E** and **R** scores. Which is higher? Write the higher score in the space below and circle the corresponding letter:

_____          E       R

Compare your **S** and **L** scores. Which is higher? Write the higher score in the space below and circle the corresponding letter:

_____          S       L

To calculate your style adaptability score, combine your SAH and SAL scores to give you a number ranging from +30 to –30. SAH are positive numbers, SAL are negative numbers.

**STYLE ADAPTABILITY SCORE**: _____

## Your 'style'

By the time we reach our mid-to-late twenties, most people have become comfortable with a particular style or way of behaving. Understanding your own style and the styles of others can help to make meetings with other people more productive. The main objective of understanding communication style is to help you to develop style adaptability in dealing with others.

Calculating your CSI–SADI scores will show your preferred style. This should help you to understand how you might 'come across' to others. If your higher scores are:

| | |
|---|---|
| E and L your style is | Supporter |
| L and R your style is | Analyst |
| R and S your style is | Director |
| E and S your style is | Instigator |

**There is no best style!** And as you read about the four styles, you'll probably say 'I can be all of these!' And you probably can! The fact is that we all have our own preferred style, but each of us has the potential ability to adopt different styles at various times. What you have identified by completing the inventory is your 'comfort zone'.

### The four CSI–SADI communication styles

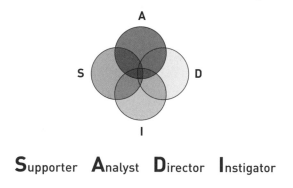

**S**upporter **A**nalyst **D**irector **I**nstigator

As you can see from the four-circle SADI diagram, there are four style comfort zones and they all overlap in the middle. At different times we can adopt any of the communication styles, but most of the time we prefer to stick to *our* comfort zone. You'll probably find that if you move out of your comfort zone, then it is easier to move to the circles either side of your comfort zone. It's usually most difficult to move to the circle that's directly opposite yours. That is because the communication style that is the direct opposite of yours is furthest from your comfort zone.

Of course there are two sides to every coin. For example, the self-confident Director may be interpreted as an insensitive steamroller by other people, and the accurate Analyst may be seen as pedantic and nitpicky. The helpful Supporter can be considered as weak and wishy-washy, while the inspiring Instigator may be seen as insincere and shallow. As you read more about your preferred style on the following pages, try to think about how other people might interpret your behaviour.

Your style can also give you some clues as to your preferred working environment. It can give some ideas on the kind of work you may prefer as well. Descriptions of the four styles are given on the following pages.

## Supporter

Supporters are 'naturals' when it comes to relating to others. You are: cooperative, a natural team player, slow-paced, trusting, quiet, supportive, friendly, a good listener, non-confrontational, sensitive, patient, understanding, generous, helpful, personable and unassuming. People see your communication style as: quiet, supportive and helpful, accommodating, loyal and able to empathise.

**You probably prefer a working environment where**: you are allowed or encouraged to think ideas over before implementing them. You are able to stand back from events and listen and watch before making decisions; you are allowed to think before acting or commenting; you can carry out research and investigate, assemble information and probe to get to the bottom of things; you are asked to produce carefully considered analyses and reports; you can reach a decision in your own time without pressure and tight deadlines; you have the opportunity for regular contact with a variety of people.

**You probably won't enjoy working where**: you are forced to stand in the limelight, such as having to act as leader/chairman/presenter; you are involved in situations that require action without planning; you are pitched into doing something without warning, such as producing an instant reaction or an instant idea; you are given insufficient data on which to base a conclusion; you are given instructions of how things should be done, without involving others; you are worried by time pressures, or rushed from one task to another; you have to take short cuts or do a superficial job.

**Questions to ask yourself**: Will I be given adequate time to consider, assimilate and prepare my work? Will there be opportunities and facilities to organise my work? Will there be opportunities to work with a wide variety of other people and incorporate their ideas into my work? Will I be under pressure to work to tight deadlines, which may result in sloppy work?

**Some job ideas**: admin assistant, bartender, coach, counsellor, diplomat, general practitioner, mediator, minister, missionary, nurse, psychologist, public relations, receptionist, salesperson, social worker, teacher.

**The strengths you'll bring to the job**: you facilitate team working and cooperation; you diffuse conflict; you create a friendly impression with people; you create a relaxed and unruffled atmosphere; you are loyal.

## Analyst

Analysts like to consider all of the options and move slowly, but precisely. You are: logical, a natural planner, quality focused, analytical, organised, exact, a perfectionist, structured, a good listener, independent, controlled, cool, non-aggressive, disciplined, deliberate and businesslike. People see your communication style as: structured and organised, quiet and unassuming, factual and logical, practical and controlled, cautious and conscientious.

**You probably prefer a working environment where**: you work within a system; you can methodically explore the associations and interrelationships between ideas, events and situations; you have the chance to question and probe the basic methodology, assumptions or logic, such as checking a report for inconsistencies; you work with high-calibre people who ask searching questions, which stretch you intellectually; you are in structured situations with a clear purpose; you are required to understand and participate in complex situations.

**You probably won't enjoy working where**: you have to do things without a context or apparent purpose, doing things just for the fun of it; you have to work in situations that focus on emotions and feelings; you are involved in unstructured work where there is a lot of ambiguity and uncertainty; you have to make decisions without guidelines or policies; you find the work shallow or gimmicky and without real purpose; you have to work with people of a lower intellectual calibre.

**Questions to ask yourself**: Will there be lots of opportunities to question my work? Is the work clear, structured and purposeful? Will I work on complex ideas and concepts that are likely to stretch me? Are the working systems tested, sound and valid?

**Some job ideas**: accountant, building inspector, business analyst, city planner, computer programmer, data processor, efficiency expert, engineer, investigator, IT/technical salesperson, Justice of the Peace, military strategist, museum curator, proofreader, quality control inspector, researcher, secretary, administrator, solicitor, surgeon, statistician.

**The strengths you'll bring to the job**: your attention to detail and production of top-quality work; logical and analytical work methods; the ability to do tedious work, for long periods, alone.

## Director

Directors prefer to be in control of situations. You are: businesslike, a natural leader, goal-centred, fast-paced, task-oriented, assertive, decisive, confident, determined, competitive, independent, straightforward, direct, an achiever, challenging, correct, you take the initiative, confront, are quick, opportunistic and forceful. People see your communication style as: in-charge, efficient, direct, quick and controlled.

**You probably prefer a working environment where**: you are given autonomy in decision making; you are in charge; you have the chance to try out and practise things, and get feedback from someone you respect because of their expertise; you respect your boss as an expert; you can implement your ideas quickly; you work on practical issues, such as drawing up action plans, suggesting short cuts and giving tips; you learn techniques for doing things with obvious practical advantages, such as how to do a job more quickly, how to make a good first impression, or how to deal with awkward people.

**You probably won't enjoy working where**: you find the work irrelevant, esoteric or unrelated to an immediate need; you cannot see the results of your efforts; you cannot see immediate relevance or practical benefits; you feel colleagues are out of touch with reality, who are pompous, or live in ivory towers; there is no practice or clear guidelines on how to do it; people go round in circles without getting anywhere; there are lots of politics and protocols; you can't see a relationship between your work and the real world.

**Questions to ask yourself**: Will I be given a free rein to do things my way? Will there be lots of practical help and resources? Does the job address real issues? Will I have a boss who knows how to/can do it? Will I be stretched?

**Some job ideas**: business coach, business manager, conductor, director, foreman, head waiter, military officer, negotiator, own business, personnel manager, pilot, police officer, president, project leader, sales manager, security guard, shop steward, supervisor.

**The strengths you'll bring to the job**: you can take charge and set goals; you can finish a lot of jobs quickly and work to tight deadlines; you take control and don't shy away from conflict.

# Instigator

Instigators like to get things going and then move on. You are: inspiring, a natural risk-taker, ideas-driven, creative, innovative, flexible, visionary, spontaneous, enthusiastic, free-spirited, energising, emotional, friendly, sociable, intuitive, an initiator, political, excitable and a doer. People see your communication style as: comforting and fun, people-centred, ambitious and competitive; inspiring and exciting; motivating.

**You probably prefer a working environment where**: there are new experiences, problems and opportunities; you can immerse yourself in short projects with tight deadlines; the environment is exciting and things change regularly with a range of diverse activities to tackle; you have a lot of the limelight/high visibility, such as chairing meetings, leading discussions and giving presentations; you are allowed to generate ideas without constraints of policy or structure; you are thrown in at the deep end with a difficult problem; you are involved with other people brainstorming ideas and solving problems, as part of a team; you feel you are free to 'have a go', to try new ideas and ways of doing things.

**You probably won't enjoy working where**: you have a passive role, with no involvement in decision making; you are required to assimilate, analyse and interpret lots of data; you have to work alone most of the time; you have to work on theoretical concepts; you have to repeat the same activity over and over again; you have precise instructions, policies and procedures to follow with little room for your interpretation; you are required to do a pedantic job and attend to lots of detail.

**Questions to ask yourself**: Will I learn something new in the job that I didn't know or couldn't do before? Will there be a wide variety of different activities? Will it be OK to have a go, let my hair down, make mistakes and have some fun? Will I work on tough problems and challenges? Will I get a chance to demonstrate my success?

**Some job ideas**: activities leader, advertising account executive, architect, artist, builder, business strategist, chief executive, estate agent, events director, explorer, headhunter, landscaper, performer, presenter, project director, property developer, public relations, tour guide, writer.

**The strengths you'll bring to the job**: your creative ideas and talents; versatility and an ability to win people over; innovative and unconventional thinking; free-spirited risk-taking; an ability to act quickly.

## The four CSI–SADI communication styles

| Supporters | Analysts |
|---|---|
| <ul><li>Need cooperation, personal security and acceptance</li><li>Are uncomfortable with and will avoid conflict</li><li>Value personal relationships, helping others and being liked</li><li>May sacrifice their own desires to win approval from others</li><li>Prefer to work with other people in a team effort, rather than individually</li><li>Have an unhurried reaction time and prefer the status quo</li><li>Are friendly, supportive, respectful, willing, dependable and agreeable</li><li>Are people-oriented</li><li>Use opinions and stories rather than facts and data</li><li>Speak slowly and softly</li><li>Lean back while talking and do not make direct eye contact</li><li>Have an informal posture and an animated expression</li><li>Are perceived as conforming, unsure, pliable, dependent and awkward</li><li>Have homely offices – family photographs, plants, etc.</li></ul> | <ul><li>Are concerned with being organised, having all the facts and being careful before taking action</li><li>Need to be accurate and to be right</li><li>Are precise, orderly and methodical and conform to standard operating procedures, organisational rules and historical ways of doing things</li><li>Have a slow reaction time and work slowly and carefully</li><li>Are perceived as serious, industrious, persistent and exacting</li><li>Are task-oriented</li><li>Use facts and data</li><li>Tend to speak slowly and want lots of information</li><li>Lean back while talking and use their hands infrequently and do not make direct eye contact</li><li>Control their facial expressions</li><li>May be seen as stuffy, indecisive, critical, picky and moralistic</li><li>Are comfortable in positions in which they can check facts and figures and be sure they are right</li><li>Have neat/well-organised offices</li></ul> |
| **Instigators** | **Directors** |
| <ul><li>Enjoy involvement, excitement and action</li><li>Are social, stimulating and enthusiastic and are good at involving and motivating others</li><li>Have ideas and are future-oriented</li><li>Have little concern for routine</li><li>Have a quick reaction time</li><li>Need to be accepted by others</li><li>Tend to be spontaneous, outgoing and energetic</li><li>Focus on people rather than tasks</li><li>Use opinions and stories rather than facts and data</li><li>Speak and act quickly; vary vocal inflection</li><li>Lean forward, point and make direct eye contact</li><li>Use their hands when talking</li><li>Have a relaxed body posture and an animated expression</li><li>Show their feelings in their faces</li><li>Are perceived by others as excitable, impulsive, undisciplined, dramatic, manipulative, ambitious, overly reactive and egotistical</li><li>Have disorganised offices that may have leisure equipment such as golf clubs or tennis racquets</li></ul> | <ul><li>Are action- and goal-oriented</li><li>Need to see results</li><li>Have a quick reaction time and are decisive, independent, disciplined, practical and efficient</li><li>Use facts and data</li><li>Speak and act quickly</li><li>Lean forward and point and make direct eye contact</li><li>Have a rigid body posture</li><li>Have controlled facial expressions</li><li>Do not want to waste time on personal talk or preliminaries</li><li>Are perceived as dominating or harsh and severe in pursuit of a goal</li><li>Are comfortable in positions of power and control</li><li>Have businesslike offices with certificates and commendations on the wall</li></ul> |

## Style adaptability

There is no 'best' style. The key to using this process is *style adaptability*. Around a quarter of the population have a similar 'style' to yours and so you will probably find that you are comfortable with them. You have probably noticed that some people are naturally very adaptable and are easily able to accommodate the needs of other people. Others are less skilled and are often seen as inflexible, or maybe even downright difficult!

By developing your adaptability skills, you will be able get on with more people. Why is this so important? As a private individual you have complete freedom of choice in whom you socialise with, whom you like and whom you don't like.

> by developing your adaptability skills, you will be able get on with more people

But to be successful at work you *must* have the skills to get along with all kinds of different people. If you know what makes *you* tick, and also have an insight into what makes your subordinates, colleagues and managers tick, then you've made a pretty good start on the journey!

The people you probably find it most difficult to relate to naturally are your 'opposites'. Study the characteristics of your opposite style. Think about how *you* can adapt your behaviour (i.e. improve your style adaptability) next time you meet someone with your 'opposite style'. For example, Analysts may need to warm up when dealing with Instigators and be prepared to be interviewed over a pie and a pint – just because the surroundings are informal does not make the meeting any less important. Instigators need to be specific and factual in their contacts with Analysts – they should be precise about what they say and give them time to assimilate it, and make decisions. Supporters need to get to the point when dealing with Directors – all that chit-chat about family and hobbies can be lost on Directors. Directors need to slow things down and indulge in friendly conversation when meeting Supporters in order to develop a trusting relationship.

## Style adaptability is a skill

Now transfer your style adaptability score from the inventory earlier in this chapter onto the scale here.

| +30 | +25 | +20 | +15 | +10 | +5 | –5 | –10 | –15 | –20 | –25 | –30 |
|-----|-----|-----|-----|-----|----|----|-----|-----|-----|-----|-----|
| **High** | | | | | | **0** | | | | | **Low** |

Style adaptability is a skill, which can be learned and developed. Some people are 'naturally' more adaptable than others. By being more adaptable you'll make other people feel more comfortable about being in your company. Your score is not fixed – you can develop your style adaptability, and the more you adapt, the easier it becomes to get on with different people. How did you score?

## Low score (0 to –30)

This may mean that you are reluctant to 'bend' to the needs of others – your approach is 'take me as I am', or 'what you see is what you get'. You like to do things for *your* reasons, rather than other people's. You hide behind your job title and use your 'position power' to get things done, rather than use the 'personal power' of your influencing skills. You may be predictable and have a low sensitivity to differences between people, which causes you to act in a predictable way. Your presence may make other people uncomfortable.

## High score (+20 to +30)

This may mean that you are very willing to adapt to meet the needs of other people. You easily see other people's reasons for doing things. You don't hide behind your job title, but use the 'personal power' of your influencing skills, rather than the power of your position. You can be unpredictable. You spend more time thinking about what makes other people happy than what makes you happy.

Of course life isn't black and white, and the above descriptions apply to the two absolute ends of the adaptability scale. Unless you scored +30, think about what I have just said. Look back at your answers to the inventory. Ask yourself the question: 'What can I do to improve my style adaptability?'

Style adaptability is a skill, which can be learned and developed. Being aware of your preferred style and understanding your style adaptability can help you to develop better relationships.

## Making the most of yourself

You should use the information you have learned about your behavioural style when you complete your CV and also when you are completing application forms. You may also like to take the on-line personality profile at: **www.keirsey.com**.

## Skills audit

We're now ready to look at the second step of the ASK process. Look at the three skills banks below and use a highlighter or tick the skills you believe you have, are good at and enjoy doing. These exercises can take a little while to complete. Do some initial work and then come back to them. Brainstorm with your partner or a close friend. It is worthwhile! Your transferable skills and knowledge bank is the vault holding the currency to obtain your next job. As you work through these exercises keep thinking of specific examples and how you can expand from the 'general' to the 'specific'. For example, if one of your skills is 'writing', then a good example might be that report you did for senior management that swayed a board meeting, or that short story you had published. Time invested on this exercise will reap its rewards when you write your CV, apply for jobs and attend interviews. You will find that you can easily and quickly identify those top skills and knowledge that you have and, importantly, articulate them to a potential employer whether in writing or at an interview.

## My transferable skills in dealing with people

I am good at and enjoy:

| | | | | |
|---|---|---|---|---|
| accepting | discovering | informing | planning | sewing |
| achieving | displaying | initiative-taking | playing | shaping |
| acting | dissecting | inspecting | preparing | showing |
| addressing | dramatising | inspiring | presenting | singing |
| administering | drawing | instructing | problem solving | sketching |
| advising | driving | integrating | processing | speaking |
| amusing | empathising | interpreting | promoting | studying |
| analysing | empowering | interviewing | protecting | summarising |
| arbitrating | encouraging | investigating | providing | supervising |
| arranging | enforcing | judging | publicising | supplying |
| assessing | enthusing | keeping fit | purchasing | symbolising |
| auditing | establishing | leading | questioning | synergising |
| budgeting | estimating | learning | raising | synthesising |
| building | evaluating | lecturing | reasoning | systematising |
| caring | examining | listening | recommending | taking |
| chairing | experimenting | maintaining | reconciling | instructions |
| charting | explaining | making | recording | talking |
| checking | expressing | inventories | recruiting | teaching |
| classifying | financing | managing | referring | team-building |
| coaching | fixing | manipulating | rehabilitating | telephoning |
| communicating | following | mediating | relating | telling |
| conducting | founding | meeting | remembering | tending |
| consolidating | gathering | memorising | repairing | testing |
| consulting | giving | miming | reporting | tolerating |
| controlling | guiding | modelling | representing | ambiguity |
| conversing | handling | monitoring | researching | training |
| coordinating | having | motivating | resolving | translating |
| coping | responsibility | negotiating | responding | treating |
| counselling | heading | observing | restoring | troubleshooting |
| creating | healing | offering | retrieving | tutoring |
| cultivating | helping | operating | risking | umpiring |
| debating | identifying | organising | scheduling | understanding |
| deciding | problems | originating | screening | understudying |
| defining | illustrating | overseeing | selecting | undertaking |
| delivering | imagining | painting | self- | uniting |
| detailing | implementing | performing | understanding | updating |
| detecting . | improving | persuading | selling | upgrading |
| developing | improvising | photographing | sensing | using |
| diagnosing | increasing | piloting | serving | |
| directing | influencing | pioneering | setting goals | |

# My transferable skills in dealing with things

I am good at and enjoy:

| | | | | |
|---|---|---|---|---|
| achieving | dispensing | illustrating | piloting | retrieving |
| adapting | displaying | implementing | planning | reviewing |
| addressing | disproving | improving | playing | salvaging |
| administering | dissecting | improvising | precision | scheduling |
| analysing | distributing | informing | predicting | sculpting |
| arranging | drawing | innovating | preparing | selecting |
| assembling | driving | inspecting | prescribing | selling |
| auditing | editing | integrating | printing | sensing |
| building | eliminating | interpreting | problem solving | separating |
| carving | emptying | inventing | processing | serving |
| checking | enforcing | investigating | programming | setting goals |
| chiselling | establishing | judging | projecting | setting-up |
| classifying | estimating | keeping | promoting | sewing |
| cleaning | evaluating | lifting | proofreading | shaping |
| collecting | examining | logging | protecting | showing |
| compiling | expanding | maintaining | providing | sketching |
| completing | expediting | making | publicising | solving |
| composing | experimenting | inventories | purchasing | sorting |
| conserving | extracting | managing | raising animals | studying |
| consolidating | fashioning | manipulating | reading | summarising |
| constructing | feeding | manufacturing | realising | supervising |
| controlling | filing | massaging | reasoning | supplying |
| cooking | financing | memorising | receiving | symbolising |
| coordinating | finishing | metalworking | recommending | synergising |
| crafting | fixing | minding | reconciling | synthesising |
| creating | forecasting | modelling | reconstructing | taking |
| cultivating | founding | monitoring | recording | instructions |
| cutting | gathering | motivating | recruiting | tending |
| deciding | generalising | moulding | reducing | testing and |
| delivering | generating | navigating | referring | proving |
| designing | getting | observing | rehabilitating | thinking logically |
| detecting | giving | obtaining | remembering | tolerating |
| determining | growing plants | offering | rendering | ambiguity |
| developing | hammering | operating | repairing | training animals |
| devising | handling | ordering | reporting | transcribing |
| diagnosing | having | organising | representing | translating |
| digging | responsibility | originating | researching | treating |
| directing | heading | overseeing | resolving | troubleshooting |
| disassembling | identifying | painting | responding | typing |
| discovering | problems | photographing | restoring | understanding |

## My transferable skills in dealing with concepts and information

I am good at and enjoy:

| | | | | | |
|---|---|---|---|---|---|
| accounting | diagnosing | identifying | painting | restoring | transcribing |
| adapting | digging | problems | perceiving | retrieving | translating |
| administering | discovering | illustrating | piloting | reviewing | treating |
| analysing | displaying | imagining | planning | risking | troubleshooting |
| animating | disproving | implementing | predicting | scheduling | typing |
| anticipating | dissecting | improving | preparing | searching | understanding |
| ascertaining | distributing | improvising | prescribing | selecting | undertaking |
| assembling | diverting | increasing | prioritising | selling | unifying |
| assessing | dramatising | influencing | problem solving | sensing | uniting |
| auditing | drawing | initiating | processing | separating | updating |
| budgeting | editing | innovating | programming | sequencing | upgrading |
| calculating | eliminating | inspecting | projecting | setting-up | using |
| charting | enforcing | installing | promoting | shaping | utilising |
| checking | establishing | instituting | proofreading | sharing | verbalising |
| classifying | estimating | integrating | protecting | sketching | visualising |
| collecting | evaluating | interpreting | providing | solving | weighing |
| compiling | examining | inventing | publicising | sorting | winning |
| completing | expanding | investigating | purchasing | storing | working |
| composing | experimenting | judging | questioning | studying | writing |
| computing | explaining | keeping | raising | summarising | |
| conceptualising | expressing | learning | reading | supplying | |
| conserving | extracting | logging | realising | symbolising | |
| consolidating | filing | maintaining | reasoning | synergising | |
| constructing | forecasting | making | receiving | synthesising | |
| controlling | formulating | managing time | recommending | systematising | |
| copying | founding | manipulating | reconciling | taking | |
| creating | gathering | mediating | recording | instructions | |
| deciding | generalising | memorising | reducing | telling | |
| decision making | generating | modelling | referring | tending | |
| defining | getting | monitoring | relating | testing and | |
| delivering | giving | observing | remembering | proving | |
| designing | guiding | obtaining | reporting | thinking | |
| detecting | handling | operating | representing | logically | |
| determining | having | ordering | researching | tolerating | |
| developing | responsibility | organising | resolving | ambiguity | |
| devising | hypothesising | originating | responding | training | |

Now that you have completed these skills banks, asterisk your 'top ten' on each page.

# Knowledge audit

It would be impossible to list an encyclopaedia of knowledge for you to use as a checklist, but thinking about different times in your life should trigger you to remember knowledge you have acquired.

Use the headings below to draw up a checklist of subjects you know something about and enjoy.

**Knowledge I have gained from:**

| School/college/ university e.g. basic French | Work e.g. auditing principles | Courses/apprenticeships/ military e.g. safety regulations |
|---|---|---|
| Reading books/newspapers/ magazines, e.g. *Car Values* | Computers/video e.g. internet auctions | Trial and error/self-study e.g. marketing principles |

# Start your brag box

Do you keep a 'brag box', as my friend Tony calls it? My own is a bursting box file … and, as I'm writing this, I'm reminding myself that it is overdue for updating! I can't think of a better name than the one Tony uses, so we'll call it a brag box! I'm talking about a collection point for documents logging your achievements through life.

When you come to complete your CV, or find you've got just one hour to fill in an application form in order to catch the post, you'll be glad of your brag box! Some of the things to include in your brag box (either as copies or originals) could be:

- Birth certificate
- Exam certificates
- Marriage certificate
- Children's birth certificates
- Passport (for number)
- Driving licence
- Membership certificates for professional institutes
- Licences to practise
- Career evaluations
- Testimonials
- Appraisals
- CPD (continuous professional development) file
- Degree(s)
- Examples of your work
- CV
- Personality and other evaluations
- Historical salary data
- Performance rankings, e.g. sales figures
- Special thank you letter from your boss or the MD!
- Sports certificates
- This book!

As well as the advantage of having everything in one place, you'll find your brag box useful for cheering yourself up on a wet Tuesday afternoon, when you feel as if you've telephoned everyone in the world and 'They're all in meetings'! But don't get too lost down memory lane … the meetings do end.

If you haven't got a brag box, start one now!

## Putting your brag box to work

> identifying your achievements will help you to realise that you have a wide variety of skills

Identifying your achievements will help you to realise that you have a wide variety of skills. You can use the information you develop in this exercise in CV presentation, completion of application forms and in preparing for job interviews.

Use the information in your brag box to help you to identify achievements you are proud of. Pick:

- four from the past two years;
- three from the five-year period before that.

Now think about the skills you used and what made your achievements so satisfying. The following phrases are often used in describing achievements.

---

**JOB** **Work achievements**

---

Improved productivity in _____ by _____

Successfully convinced (my manager, subordinates, etc.) to _____

Developed (introduced, designed, etc.) a new (method/system, etc.) for _____ resulting in _____

Motivated subordinates by _____

Detected a serious error in (a procedure, filing system, report, etc.) and
_____

Improved technological process (service etc.) by _____
_____

Successfully arranged and ran a meeting on _____
_____

Changed _____

Improved quality control in _____ by _____

Successfully arranged and ran a meeting on _____

Initiated and implemented a (programme campaign, process, etc.) to
_____

Increased market share of _____

---

### ⊙ JOB   Non-work achievements

Created (managed, ran, etc.) a fund-raising campaign for (name of charitable, athletic or artistic activity/group).

Successfully counselled, advised, helped a friend to _____

Organised (coordinated, etc.) a charitable drive for _____

Established (acted as secretary of) a professional association (social, athletic club, etc.) _____

Acted as a member of a committee or chaired a committee _____

As (a founding member of a local organisation) created a campaign to _____ and successfully raised funds for _____ etc.

Organised a day trip to _____ for a group of _____ (mothers and toddlers).

Did (oversaw) the decorations for _____

Successfully renovated my house myself _____

Having identified your achievements, think about the skills you used and what made the experience satisfying. Think about what you gained or learned. Make a few notes, as I have in the chart opposite. These concrete examples of experiences and transferable skills will be invaluable for completing your CV and job applications and also when you are answering questions in interviews.

| Achievement | Skills used | What made the achievement satisfying? |
| --- | --- | --- |
| Coordinated sponsored run | Conceived the campaign | Managing |
| Enlisted six volunteers to assist in organising the campaign | Managing others | Planning the campaign |
| Informed local newspaper to generate publicity | Motivating others | Running meetings |
| Ran four meetings with volunteers | Planning and organising | Contributing to something I believe in |
| Coordinated the volunteers by assigning tasks | Delegating tasks | The results – £5,000! |
| Developed plan to go to the schools to inform people about the run and enlist volunteers | Running effective meetings<br><br>Public relations – selling the campaign | Being recognised |
| Got 200 people to take part in the run | Persuading people to participate | Being in the limelight |

# Keeping your skills and knowledge up to date

'When we stop learning, we stop living.' One of the things that may come out of your skills audit is recognition that there's a gap between where you are now and where you'd like to be – a 'training gap'. Think carefully about how you'd like to close that gap by taking additional training. Go to your library or search the internet, ask at the careers service, the job centre or your local college to check out the options. Be aware of your own learning style. Some people can study alone and pass exams by reading a few books or taking a correspondence course. Others need the support of others. If you're out of work, you'll probably find that there are many courses that you can attend free of charge. Ask! And don't think you'll be the class dunce just because you haven't studied for 20 years – you'll find that others on the course had the same fear. If you need some inspiration to help you get over your anxiety, read Susan Jeffers' excellent book *Feel the Fear and Do It Anyway*.

There are very few jobs (if any) that require minimal or no skills at all, and as technology advances, the need for people with a wide variety of skills, including IT skills, increases. Peter Drucker, the management guru, predicted that 'the factories of the future will have only two employees: a person and a dog. The person's job will be to feed the dog and the dog's job will be to bite the person if they touch any of the controls or switches.' An extreme prediction, maybe, and probably something that will never happen, but an insight into the way the world of work is changing. Think about the developments and technological advances that have taken place at home and at work over the past two or three decades. When did you last see a typewriter? Do you still use a film camera? Whatever happened to the blackboard in the school classroom? Technological advances mean that new skills are constantly needed in the workplace. Training and re-training is the key to learning new skills and unlocking your own potential.

If you are having difficulty finding a new job it may be that you need a skills-makeover. You can take control of your future by deciding to improve your skills. Your chances of getting work, gaining a promotion, improving your career, starting your own business, or even being paid a higher salary will all be improved if you develop your skills. Fortunately, help is at hand. Through Learndirect you can gain access to almost a million courses throughout the country in subjects from mountain survival to catering; and Vision2Learn also has some excellent free courses that I can vouch for personally as I upgraded my IT skills through their ITQ course and it didn't cost me a penny! See the end of this section for contact details.

> your chances of getting work will be improved if you develop your skills

Re-training could give you an opportunity for a completely different career. Have a look at jobs where there are skills shortages, such as the traditional building trades – there seems to be a nationwide shortage of plumbers and electricians and their earnings are very healthy. Or what about a career in IT? Who says that just because you're over 40 you can't re-train as a web developer and guarantee yourself an income for as long as you wish to continue working?

A final word of caution: be wary of organisations offering IT courses with a pot of gold at the end of the rainbow. These are companies who charge you a substantial fee up-front for a training course with an 'offer' of 'guaranteed employment' at the end. I'm sure most are decent and honest, and will help you to get a job, but I have heard stories of people paying for courses leading to qualifications that don't mean anything to employers, and then being left to their own devices at the end of the course.

*Training providers for learning and skills development*

BBC Education Learning Zone: **www.bbc.co.uk/education/lzone**

BTEC/Edexcel Vocational Qualifications: **www.edexcel.org.uk**

City and Guilds: **www.city-and-guilds.co.uk**

Learndirect: **www.learndirect.co.uk**

Lifelonglearning: **www.lifelonglearning.co.uk**

Open University: **www.open.ac.uk/courses**

Vision2Learn: **www.vision2learn.co.uk**

# How to write your CV

**Recruiters are all different.** There is an expression that goes, 'If you are ill and ask three Harley Street specialists for a second opinion then you'll get five different opinions'! In the same way, recruiters have personal preferences in how they like to see CVs written. For this reason I can't offer dogmatic advice and say this is the way you *must* present your CV. Added to which, your CV is a very personal document – in the final analysis you are the best judge of whether your CV best represents you.

On the following pages is a 'CV summary' document which will help you to gather the relevant information and some sample CVs to help you to decide on which layout you like best. Nowadays most CVs are sent electronically so it is essential that you write it so that it is well presented both on-screen and if printed out.

## Basic principles – all CVs

- Be brief – use one or two pages if possible. You can do it! Screening of CVs is brief. If the most relevant item is on page 7, paragraph 6, forget it! And PLEASE, PLEASE don't use more pages than you need to! One or two, or maybe three if you must, but don't go on to 28 pages, as I saw with one candidate. Honestly!

- Use a legible font – and stick to one font (or two at the most if you want to incorporate a contrast). The fonts without the bobbly bit, such as New Courier and Veranda, shown below, are called sans-serif (sans = French for without); the serifs on fonts such as Times New Roman are there to help your eye to move quickly as you read. If your CV is a long document, with lots of information, you might choose to use a font with serifs. If it's short and you want the reader to savour every word, use a sans-serif font.

  This is in 8 point Times New Roman PS

  This is in 10 point New Courier

  **This is in 12 point Veranda**

- Beware of jargon! – write in plain English if you are a logistics manager, a military officer, a research scientist, etc. Indeed, if you are a specialist of any kind, you will almost certainly have your own vocabulary. Use plain English!

- Be specific – 'I have five years' experience in …' says far more than 'I have wide experience of …', as does 'I reduced inventory from £4.2m to £1.8m in a period of 12 months', compared with 'We made substantial savings by reducing our inventory.' The more you can demonstrate that you achieved SMART objectives in your replies, the better you will impress the recruiter.

- Even if you can produce a decent letter, it may be worth investing in getting someone to do your CV for you. If you need help with the content then you may need a professional CV writer. On the other hand, a professionally trained secretary can do wonders in terms of improving the presentation. Local newspapers, newsagents' windows and, of course, the internet are a good source. There are thousands of 'professional CV writers' on the internet. If you decide to get help, ask to see previous examples and make sure they give you a copy of the file for future updating and so that you can 'personalise' key strengths to produce a targeted CV to fit each job. If you decide to use the internet to find someone then stick to your own country; I was born in the UK and have lived here for most of my life, but at times I have lived in Australia and in the USA. While I could communicate with the 'natives', I'd be stretching it to say that we spoke the same language! Of course, if you are applying for a job in the USA then it may be advantageous to use an American CV writer.

- Some of the modern software packages have CV templates, but before you decide to use a template, make sure that you're comfortable with the style, layout and content. It's your CV. And remember, if you're using the CV builder that came with your word processor it may end up looking just the same as all the other applicants using the same software. There are also some inexpensive commercially available CV-writing software packages that use a menu to ask a long series of questions and then produce a CV based on your answers. These can be found by searching Amazon or eBay.

- If you're applying for your first job, or are returning to work after bringing up a family, help the recruiter to recognise your transferable skills. 'President of the outdoor pursuits society' and 'qualified mountain leader' implies leadership and someone trained to cope with adversity. 'Treasurer of the parish church council' implies financial skills and abilities to deal with contractors, etc. Spell it out for them.

- Proofread, proofread, proofread. Start at the bottom of the page and read backwards. You may thimk there are no mistakes, but by reading backwards you see each word in isolation and can spot errors and misspellings. For example, did you spot 'thimk' in the last sentence or did you read what you thought was there?

> proofread, proofread, proofread

- Use short paragraphs of only 3–4 sentences. This makes documents more visually appealing by adding white space and makes it easier for the reader to absorb the information.

- Headings: use a larger/bold font to provide headings to paragraphs.

## Basic principles – electronic CVs

- Incorporate white space into the text; reading large blocks of text on a computer screen can be difficult.

- Put the most important information in your CV at the top of the first page so that it can be seen on the screen when the document is open. If your opening paragraphs don't make the sales pitch and grab the recruiter's attention, they are unlikely to scroll down to read the rest.

- Use bullet points and lists to break up the text and summarise. This makes it easier for the reader to absorb the information in your CV.

- Use hyperlinks to link to relevant sites that will support your application; e.g. your previous employer's website, your LinkedIn profile or your presentations at SlideShare.net. Populate the CV with correctly spelled keywords. Organisations use computers to 'crawl' over CVs to look for words that 'match' the criteria they have set as requirements for employees. If you repeat the keywords from their job description and person specification in your CV you'll be moved up the selection chain.

## Basic principles – printed CVs

- Use clean, laser-printed or quality ink-jet originals; not photocopies of photocopies!

- Use good-quality paper of 90 or 100 gsm. Either use a quality high white or a softer Old English white. Avoid pretty pastel shades!

- Presentation 'gimmicks' – personally I like to receive CVs from people who have had them bound or who have included a photograph. It says that they are prepared to put that bit of extra effort into their application. I know, however, that many of my fellow human resources professionals would strongly disagree. Your decision has to be based on the job and what you know about the organisation.

- Print your CV single-sided – if only because it makes it easier to photocopy!

- If you have a name that may be interpreted as either male or female, such as Jay or Frankie, enter 'm' or 'f' in brackets. I'm certainly not advocating sexual discrimination in recruitment, but it puts recruiters off-balance when they phone candidates and get their sex wrong! If you think your name might cause confusion, help recruiters by explaining. Name: Malcolm (given) Hornby (family). And if you were named Rebecca at birth and have since then been known only as Becky, then put Becky on your CV. Remember it's *your* marketing tool.

- Some recruiters like a wide margin on the left-hand side so that they can make notes.

- CVs often get separated from letters of application. Use the header and footer facility to ensure that your name and address are on each page – it will help if pages do become separated. It will also help an interviewer to remember your name when they are halfway through an interview and they've turned over the page!

## What language should you use in CVs?

'It ain't what you say, it's the way that you say it.' This is not totally true, but there is an element of truth to it! Striking a balance between being positive and sounding arrogant can be a real challenge.

Use active words and not passive words. 'I was responsible for managing a project team that installed a new intranet' says more than 'I was involved in installing a new intranet.' The first statement is far more powerful, while the second might mean no more than you plugged it in and switched it on!

Avoid passive words, such as liaised with, coordinated and administered. Use some of the following action verbs when writing your CV and also for letters of application.

## Action verbs

| | | | |
|---|---|---|---|
| accelerated | extended | reduced | traced |
| accomplished | finished | reorganised | traded |
| achieved | generated | revised | trained |
| approved | implemented | scheduled | transferred |
| completed | improved | serviced | translated |
| conceived | increased | set up | trimmed |
| conducted | introduced | simplified | tripled |
| consolidated | launched | sold | turned |
| created | maintained | solved | uncovered |
| decided | negotiated | started | united |
| delivered | ordered | streamlined | utilised |
| demonstrated | performed | strengthened | vacated |
| designed | pioneered | stressed | waged |
| developed | planned | stretched | widened |
| directed | processed | structured | won |
| doubled | programmed | succeeded | worked |
| eliminated | promoted | summarised | wrote |
| ended | proposed | superseded | |
| established | purchased | supervised | |
| expanded | redesigned | terminated | |

But beware – don't overdo it. The recruiter is looking for a mortal!

Try reading the finished version of your CV to your partner or close friend. If you go a little pink you're probably spot on – bright red and you've overdone it!

## How to avoid convoluted and imprecise expressions – 'brevity is best'

| Avoid | Use |
|---|---|
| As a result of this project the company's costs were cut by ... | This cut costs by ... |
| During the period referred to in the previous sentence ... | I ... |
| As a consequence of the success of this project, I was asked to take up the more senior appointment of ... | I was promoted ... |
| In this position I ... | I ... |
| Considerable elements of my responsibilities were ... | I was responsible for ... |
| anticipate | expect |
| behind schedule | late |
| prior to | before |
| personnel | people |
| proceeded to | then |
| inaugurated | set up |
| initiated | started |
| terminated | ended |

## CV checklist

This checklist combines the **should be (bold)** and *could be (italic)* included items. Use this in combination with the CV summary below to help you to gather information and to develop your own CV.

- **Name, address, e-mail and telephone number(s) stating daytime contact.**

- *Marital status.*

- *Number of dependants and ages.*

- *Nationality.*

- *Date of birth/age.*

- **School, college/university attended – normally only from age of 11 onwards, unless you're a school leaver or recent graduate.**

- **Qualifications – for a school leaver or recent graduate looking for a first job state GCSEs and GCEs (level, subjects and pass grade) along with subjects taken and class of degree. For a 45-year-old divisional director, 6 O levels, 3 A levels, BSc 2(i) Chemistry is usually sufficient, although for some professions, for example accountancy, you may wish to include GCE A level grades.**

- *Language proficiency.*

- *Willingness to relocate – especially if you're out of commuting distance (omit if you aren't).*

- **Current/last job – state this first, then work backwards through your career, allocating most space to recent job(s) with brief mentions of your early career. Give a one- or two-sentence summary of the company products/ services and their annual turnover and summarise your responsibilities and achievements against each job.**

- *Current/last salary and benefits package, for example company car. Be brief. Opinions differ on whether salary should be included – you may wish to keep your cards close to your chest and risk missing an opportunity because they think you'll be 'too expensive'.*

- *Career aims.*

- *Personal strengths.*

- *Leisure activities; be realistic – a one-week skiing holiday five years ago does not qualify you as a skier! Include a variety to show that you have broad interests, but not too many – they may think you'll have no time left for work! Three to four interests should be adequate.*

- *Professional achievements – for example titles of research papers or articles you have had published. But don't, like someone who once sent me a 28-page CV, attach the papers!*

- *Memberships of professional institutions and whether by examination or election.*

- *Do not include names of referees, unless you are applying for a job in the public sector.*

- *Driving licence – clean and current don't mean the same!*

## JOB CV summary

**Name:**    **Address:**    **Tel. and e-mail:**

**Strengths** – four or five short sentences about your personal strengths. A four- or five-sentence summary of your career, who you are and what you have to offer. Make every word count!

**Education and qualifications** – place right here up front if you have a first class honours degree, PhD, MBA. You may wish to leave to the end if your business achievements outshine your academic ones!

**Career history** – most recent first and work backwards. Include responsibilities and quantified achievements. Reduce the information as you go back – for example, give five achievements for your current/most recent job, three from a job two years ago, but only one from a job 15 years ago.

**Professional memberships, etc.**

**Personal information** – willingness to relocate, interests, marital status, etc. Add only as much as you believe you need to. Your personal information is not deemed as having any relevance to whether you can or can't do a job.

## Is it worth using 'ready-made' templates

Many of today's word-processing packages contain excellent pre-formatted CV templates, but beware of their limitations (see earlier in this chapter). There are also lots of ideas to be had from the job sites on the internet, as well as CV-builder websites. Experiment with the different styles and formats until you find one that you're most comfortable with. A Google search for 'CV builder' will also give you lots of options.

## Are you leaving the forces – or any highly technical environment?

Mind your language when writing your CV! Now what do I mean by that? All professions have their own jargon and expressions. If you're an accountant looking for a job as an accountant, you can talk to an interviewer in accountant-speak, or a surgeon talking to another surgeon ... and so on. If you are 'stepping out' into civvy street you'll need to use a different language to the one you're used to using.

To give you an example. I live in Lincolnshire and there are four RAF bases within a 15-minute drive. I even get my own private air show occasionally when the Red Arrows practise over my house! Recently, I was asked to give advice on the CV of a friend of a friend who is leaving the RAF. The first thing that struck me was his rank/job title of 'technician' – there was no further explanation. A chat over the phone revealed that he's a highly skilled, highly qualified engineer and is responsible (along with others) for making sure that about 40 million pounds' worth of aircraft works as it should. Years ago I used to be involved in recruiting semi-skilled 'manufacturing technicians', who were process workers on a shampoo production line. Have I made my point?

Prospective employers may have little or no knowledge of the specialist skills and attributes that you use in your service role, or the ways in which these can be transferred across to civilian jobs. As a result of this, they may be reluctant to take you on as an unknown quantity.

When you write your CV and letters of application, and when you go to interviews, make sure that you explain what your current job involves, along with your responsibilities, in plain English that can be understood by non-specialists.

**stress your transferable skills**

Stress your transferable skills. This is especially important if you have to send your CV to a personnel department or a recruitment agency. The people responsible for the initial screening are often non-specialists, involved in recruiting people for many different kinds of jobs.

If you have served in the armed forces at any time in your life, the following may be able to help you in your job hunt:

- Regular Forces Employment Association – tel: 020 7321 2011 for your local branch, or **www.rfea.org.uk.**

- The Officers' Association – tel: 020 7930 0125, or **www.officersassociation.org.uk.**

- SSAFA Forces Help – tel: 020 7403 8783 for your local branch, or **www.ssafa.org.uk.**

# Examples of CVs/résumés

If you're sitting in front of a blank computer screen saying 'where do I begin?', then I hope the following pages of sample CVs will help you to write your own.

None of the examples should be taken as definitive. Each is unique to the person who wrote it. They are CVs from real people and each of them has 'worked' because it helped the writer to *Get That Job!* I hope that you will be able to take learning points from each to enable you to develop your own unique, personal and effective CV. Use the table below to help summarise the most useful points. Make a note of things you like and things you'd like to avoid in your CV. Remember, it's *your cv*. It's not a confessional – it's a marketing tool.

(Please note that names and places of work on the CVs have been changed for confidentiality.)

| Learning points from other people's CVs | |
|---|---|
| Things I like – to be used in my CV | Things I don't like – to be avoided in my CV |
| | |

**Note**: it is a good idea to print your CV single-sided – if only because it makes it easier to photocopy!

STEVEN JOHNSON
22 Coventry Road, Edgbaston
Birmingham B66 77BM
Home tel: (0303) 30303
E-mail: Steven@Johnson.oc.ku

Highly motivated, energetic senior manager, having successfully achieved objectives through developing people. A natural leader, with strong interpersonal and communication skills, who thrives on being involved in leading teams in an environment of creativity and constant challenge. Responsible for results of a keenly focused team in terms of sales, quality and profitability. Displays initiative and a positive outlook to all challenges, an ideas generator, decisive and highly adaptable to change. Extensive experience and knowledge of both general and sales management, with an in-depth understanding of the people business.

ACHIEVEMENTS

Developed teams of managers, monitoring both personal performance and that of the sales units, ensuring objectives achieved, together with quality and service standards being maintained.

Created a competitive team spirit whereby individual and collective performance was recognised. Provided league tables, instigated competitions, produced interesting and varied communication formats.

Energised team, created environment ensuring national sales campaigns were tackled enthusiastically, with success being achieved and measured in improving performance position. Appointed and managed new direct sales force, including sales meetings, one-to-one coaching and field visits. Developed and nurtured relationships with sales units to achieve common business objectives, resulting in business levels being increased by 140% over a six-month period.

Produced quarterly/annual business plans to ensure focus and direction to achieving business and quality objectives.

Instigated and developed a programme and systems for achieving total quality management, resulting in customer service complaints being reduced by 28% in three months.

Responsible for staff recruitment at junior management level, disciplinary matters and general personnel responsibilities, including managing staff budgets.

Responsible for quarterly/annual appraisal process whereby individuals recognise critical success factors that are incorporated within a personal development plan.

Involved with the training of staff, both within units and at the area training centre. Follow-up process adopted to ensure training benefits maximised.

Took part in strategic projects from inception to final presentation, enabling project management skills to be developed to the full.

Conducted regular meetings and one-to-one discussions using consultative planning approach, agreeing action points to ensure progress.

STEVEN JOHNSON ctd

| CAREER PROGRESSION | 1986–present | Stable Building Society |
|---|---|---|
| 2011–present | **Area Sales Manager** | Midlands |
| | Responsible for 16 managers, 135 staff | |
| | Report to the Area Sales Director | |
| 2010–2011 | **Regional Sales Manager** | East Midlands |
| | Responsible for 8 managers, 4 direct sales | |
| 2009–2010 | **Regional Manager** | Coventry |
| 2008–2009 | **Assistant Regional Manager** | Coventry |
| 2007–2008 | **Branch Manager** | Harrogate |
| 2000–2007 | **Branch Manager** | Crewe |
| 1994–2000 | **Branch Manager** | Maidenhead |
| 1986–1994 | **Junior Management/Senior Clerical** | Various locations |

PERSONAL DEVELOPMENT

| March 2004 | Sundridge Park Management Centre |
|---|---|
| November 2000 | Peters Management Consultants (sales training) |
| December 1988 | Ashridge Management College (extensive internal training covering a wide range of topics) |

ADDITIONAL INFORMATION

Married – 1 child (19)
Fellow Chartered Building Society Institute
School governor/chairman of charitable trust
Past member of Round Table, holding a number of offices including chairman
Computer literate – all Microsoft Office software packages

INTERESTS

Gardening, golf, badminton, stamp collecting, trying to keep fit

PETER RADLETT
14 Greenview
Central Milton Keynes
MK98 89MK
Tel: (987) 676767 Mobile: 1000 6987654
E-mail: Peter@Radlett.oc.ku

CAREER PROFILE

Experienced and versatile manager with strong leadership skills. Knowledge of high technology applied to a variety of product-based organisations. Commercially aware. Adept at introducing change, either in the organisation or by the introduction of capital investment, and who recognises that high productivity is only achieved through a knowledgeable and motivated team.

ACHIEVEMENTS

- Implemented a £4-million investment programme on a greenfield site through the installation and commissioning of four discrete product lines.
- Implemented capital investment programme to reduce reliance on external suppliers of key components.
- Introduced the concept of operator process control by use of a series of training modules.
- Recruited, trained and motivated the production team to develop and grow the business.
- Implemented new production planning routines to reduce generation of works documentation from 10 days to 4 days.
- Reduced inventory holding on major product lines from 15 weeks to 5 weeks.
- Developed, through training, line management supervision.
- Reduced losses by improved monitoring and feedback to suppliers.

CAREER HISTORY

| | |
|---|---|
| 2011–Present | OPMKS Ltd, Milton Keynes – Manufacturing Manager, responsible to Operations Director, for all aspects of manufacture for photographic enlargers in a vertically integrated organisation |
| 2010–2011 | TISSUE Group, Hemel Hempstead – Production Manager, responsible to Operations Director, for all aspects of manufacture for Tissue Culture Products |
| 2008–2010 | VENTILATORS Ltd, High Wycombe – Production Manager, responsible to Manufacturing Director, for line production, line planning and stock control |
| 2002–2008 | HYDRAULIC MOTORS Ltd, High Wycombe – Manufacturing Manager, responsible to General Manager, for purchasing, production planning, stock control, production engineering, machining, assembly and despatch |

PETER RADLETT ctd

## EDUCATION AND QUALIFICATIONS
1991–1993      Hemel Hempstead Polytechnic – HND in Mechanical
               Engineering
2005           High Wycombe College of Further Education – Certificate in
               Computing Studies
2006           High Wycombe College of Further Education – Member,
               Institute of Industrial Managers (IIM)

## MANAGEMENT TRAINING
1980           Guardian Business School – accountancy for non-financial
               managers
2010–2011      Paradigm Shifters – leadership and decision-making skills

## INTERESTS
Squash, home improvements, computing, walking and classic cars

ROBERT GREEN
Ivybridge House
Manchester Road
Stalybridge
M99 99M
Tel: (669) 99991. Mobile: 1234 7654321. e-mail: Rob@Green.oc.ku

An experienced manager with design, technical and sales skills. Have designed numerous products, including bedroom/kitchen ranges and occasional furniture. Prepared technical details of products including packaging. Handled numerous sales enquiries/contracts, liaising with clients at all levels. Assembled and fitted products, including bedroom and kitchen ranges.

## ACHIEVEMENTS

- Designed many successful products for mail order and high street clients, including a new bedroom range by Bedroom Sellers and Housefitters.
- Handled door contracts with national companies, from enquiries through to production.
- Designed and erected exhibition stands, both in the UK and abroad.

### EXPERIENCE

**Bedrooms Ltd,**
**Manchester**                    **Development Manager**        **2010–present**

Responsible for design and development of all the company's new products from conception through to production. This involves accurate preparation of production drawings using AutoCAD, material and fittings specifications, packing design and instruction leaflets. On the sales side I handle all the company's incoming door and component enquiries, liaising closely with customers on technical matters. I have a staff of five and am responsible for CNC programming and the development workshop.

**Components Ltd,**
**Lancashire**                    **Development Manager**        **1994–2010**

Commenced my career as design draughtsperson, working my way to Development Manager on leaving. I was responsible for all aspects of design and development work, including aesthetic, economic and production considerations. Was required to draw up and meet planning timetables; producing sketches and costs for short-listed designs. Was involved with presentation and selling of product, pricing and quotations. I produced detailed customer assembly leaflets and was responsible for a busy development workshop.

**Shell Oil Refinery,**
**Cheshire**                    **Process Operator**        **1991–1994**

Responsible for efficient running of petrol refinery plant.

**Bolton Borough Council, Bolton    Clerk/Draughtsman         1986–1991**

I gained experience in several different aspects of a council department, including printing, preparation of artwork and furniture design. I planned kitchen layouts for home economics rooms in schools and colleges.

<u>EDUCATION AND TRAINING</u>

**Bolton Technical High School**

GCE O levels in English Language, Mathematics and Technical Drawing

**Manchester College of Furniture**

Trained for design and construction of furniture

**FIRA**

Various day courses and seminars

**Bolton College of Further Education**

City and Guilds in computer-aided draughting and design using AutoCAD

<u>HOBBIES AND PASTIMES</u>

I am a married man with two children. My interests include most sports, but particularly fishing. I live close to moorland and do a lot of walking. I maintain and improve our house and do most of my own car maintenance.

CATHERINE SCARLET
14 Severn View, Bristol, BS99 9AA
Tel: 1234 56789 (home), 1234 98765 (mobile)
E-mail: Catherine@Scarlet.oc.ku

Finance director with general management, company development and acquisition experience, combined with practical operating skills in the investment banking, broking, chemical processing and retail distribution industries. Special abilities include:

- Managing change, turning round underperforming activities.
- Forming, managing and motivating teams, developing individuals.
- Developing profitable relationships, negotiating business deals.
- Analysing, evaluating and managing company acquisitions.

CAREER
**Lotsacash Investment Bank Group, 2008–present**
Operations Director, Capital Markets & Treasury
- Responsible for efficient operation of capital markets/treasury financial control, settlements and computer operations. 100 staff, budget £10m.
- I was headhunted to turn round ineffective accounting, computer and treasury control system.
- Rebuilt teams, improved staff quality and training, reduced staff and overtime without disruption, significantly improved management information and operating efficiency.
- Investigated and negotiated joint-venture arrangements in Europe.

**Broking International plc, 1999–2008**
Commercial Director, 2007–2008
- Responsible for the London-based broking businesses. T/O £75m, profit £9m, 500 staff.
- Conducted start-up of German bond-broking business.

Financial Director, Management and Securities Division, 2002–2007
- Responsible for advising the Board on worldwide financial and related management matters. T/O £113m, profit £22m, 90 staff.
- Close involvement with acquisitions in UK, USA, Germany, Luxembourg, Hong Kong, Singapore and Australia and with subsequent business development.

Group Financial Controller, 1999–2002
- Improved full range of management systems and controls in media advertising and broking exercises.
- Contributions in the job led to promotion to Financial Director.

**Stackem High Stores, 1998–1999**
Internal consultant, Retail Stores Division
- Investigated, recommended and implemented the integration of two stores groups.

CATHERINE SCARLET ctd

**Springy Sofas Ltd, 1997**
Managing Director
- Planned and brought new factory to full production of moulded urethane components.
- Developed market strategy and customer base of group. T/O £3m, profit £160k.

QUALIFICATIONS
BA Accountancy and Law 2/1, University of Bristol 1989
CA gained with Price Waterhouse, 1992

PERSONAL
Age 46 years. Married, two children. Health excellent. Interests – family, antiques, aerobics, Greek mythology (launched and maintain special-interest internet community website: *www.GreekGeeks.co.uk*).

JANET WAITE
58 Desmond Road
London
NW19 9DE
Tel: (020) 055 5656, Mobile: 09876544567890. e-mail: JWAITE@ssd.moc

PROFILE

An effective personnel generalist with skills in team-building and gaining commitment from senior management through persuasion.

Enjoys deadlines and performs well under pressure. Gives wholehearted commitment to a task and displays a high degree of tenacity and resilience when facing difficult situations.

Outside the work environment enjoys being stretched and has, for example, in the last few years taken up skiing, windsurfing and paragliding.

CAREER

**Very Wealthy Banks (Investments) plc** 2007–present
Based in the City with 2,500 employees in a highly IT-oriented environment.

**Personnel Manager:** 2012–present
Settlement Services Division
A strongly generalist role, responsible for the provision of an effective professional service to c.900 staff. Managing a team of six personnel staff. My achievements in this role have been:

- Following significant cutbacks, selected to contribute to re-structuring.
- Charged with the task of detailed project planning and execution for the transfer of personnel activities back to line managers.

**Personnel Manager Information Technology** 2009–2012
Managing a team of five staff (including three professional personnel officers) covering strongly systems-development-oriented client areas, c.550 staff. My achievements in this position were:

- Worked with the senior management team to revise job roles and restructure:
  a) The Systems Development and Support department, resulting in the reduction of 30 staff and
  b) The Management Services department, resulting in the reduction of 50 jobs.
- Established a new personnel team of five from scratch – recruited, analysed training needs and coached for their improved job performance through regular meetings and improved communications. Heightened team contribution and helped them to develop in their own roles.
- Implemented psychometric testing to determine analytical skills, and assessment centre techniques to clarify project management potential, ensuring the cost-effective application of training programmes.
- Successfully implemented the appraisal policy within client area, running courses and successfully working to overcome management resistance to objective setting.

**Principal Personnel Officer: Business Development Department** 2008–2009

- In a predominantly sales and marketing environment managed three staff, in a generalist role serving staff in the south east, UK regional offices and New York, but also with emphasis on recruitment and remuneration.

JANET WAITE ctd

- Gained acceptance to the establishment of career paths for Business Development department staff, involving progress through customer support, UK sales, international sales and the New York office.
- Creative and analytical approach to recruitment into a number of key roles, according to a specification that required a unique combination of financial services, computer industry and sales/marketing expertise.

**Senior Personnel Officer**                                                            2007–2008

A generalist role, covering the Systems Development and Sales and Marketing departments. Particularly involving recruitment and development (graduate and YTS); and experience in HAY-based job evaluation. Achievements in this position were:

- Sold new salary review concepts to line managers and worked with them in resolving the remuneration-level problems that were leading to high turnover of specialist staff.
- Initiated an in-house recruitment event to appeal to computer scientists, gained the commitment of the senior management to participate in the event and achieved recruitment targets.

**Big Boat Builders, Research & Development**                                  2005–2007

Research, development and production of electronic equipment, 2,500 staff.

**Senior Personnel Officer – Recruitment**

Responsible for the recruitment of professional, technical, manual, clerical and secretarial staff. Involved in the recruitment of graduates and professional engineers. Achievements in the position were:

- Became the driving force behind the use of psychometric testing for the recruitment of specialist, high-value staff. By means of presentations to senior management gained acceptance for this approach.
- Ran a series of 'walk-in interviews' to attract scarce technical skills and validated its cost effectiveness.

**Car Parts Ltd**                                                                        2001–2005

Manufacture and distribution of automotive parts, approx. 2,500 staff.

Successive appointments in this heavily unionised environment. Trainee, Salaries and Records Administrator, Personnel Officer, Systems Coordinator, Recruitment and Salaries Adviser.

**Electronic Switching Ltd**                                                        1999–2001

Import/Export Sales Coordinator.

EDUCATION AND TRAINING

Chartered Member of the Chartered Institute of Personnel and Development (2008)
BSc Combined Hons Degree in Science (Zoology/Geography)

Psychometric Testing

Registered user of Kostic PAPI (Perception and Preference Inventory), Saville and Holdsworth (OPQ and Aptitude Tests)

PERSONAL

My interests include: windsurfing, skiing, hill walking, watching motor racing, keeping Siamese cats and going to the theatre.

## Functional or skills CVs

Chronological vs functional CVs. All of the CVs I have shown so far are traditional chronological CVs. This last example CV is a 'functional' or 'skills' CV. A chronological CV is the most common kind of CV. It's the kind of CV that tracks your career from start to finish; but it is not necessarily the best kind for older candidates or candidates who have had a gap in employment caused, say, by self-employment. The chronological CV takes the reader back step by step through your career, moving in reverse order from your current position or most recent position back (usually) to the start of your career. It is best to use a chronological CV

> the chronological CV can also demonstrate a solid career history

when the job you have applied for is a logical successor to your previous jobs. Previous jobs hopefully show that your responsibilities have increased as your experience has broadened. The chronological CV can also demonstrate a solid career history rather than the kind that shows someone with itchy feet.

The functional or skills CV puts the emphasis on your skills and experiences without being heavily biased towards a particular job. The functional CV is often recommended for older applicants or for people changing career direction. You may also consider using a functional CV if you have worked for obscure organisations, or you want to hide the fact that you were self-employed. You can also use a functional CV if you have had a lot of job changes, a long period of unemployment, or if there is no obvious career direction. You still give your job history, but briefly, in a separate section.

Janine Parks
76 Middle Road, North Park
Southwood AA66 77ZZ
HOME TEL: (0303) 30303
E-mail Janine.Parks@home.oc.ku

OBJECTIVE

To secure a senior management position within banking where my previous experience, sales, leadership and banking skills can be utilised to maximise their potential.

Highly motivated, energetic senior manager who has successfully achieved objectives through developing people. A flexible leader, with strong interpersonal and communication skills, who thrives on being involved in leading teams in an environment of creativity and constant challenge. Responsible for results of a keenly focused team in terms of sales, quality and profitability. Displays initiative and a positive outlook to all challenges, an ideas generator, decisive and highly adaptable to change. Extensive experience and knowledge of both general and sales management, with an in-depth understanding of the people business.

ACHIEVEMENTS

Developed teams of managers, monitoring both personal performance and that of the sales units, ensuring objectives achieved together with quality and service standards being maintained.

Created a competitive team spirit whereby individual and collective performance was recognised. Provided league tables, instigated competitions, produced interesting and varied communication formats.

Energised team, created environment ensuring national sales campaigns were tackled enthusiastically, with success being achieved and measured in improving performance position. Appointed and managed new direct sales force, including sales meetings, one-to-one coaching and field visits. Developed and nurtured relationships with sales units to achieve common business objectives, resulting in business levels being increased by 140% over a 6-month period.

Produced quarterly/annual business plans to ensure focus and direction to achieving business objectives.

Instigated and developed a programme and systems for achieving total quality management, resulting in customer service complaints being reduced by 28% in 3 months.

Responsible for staff recruitment at junior management level. Disciplinary matters and general personnel responsibilities, including managing staff budgets.

Responsible for quarterly/annual appraisal process whereby individuals recognise critical success factors that are incorporated within a personal development plan.

Involved with the training of staff, both within units and at Area Training Centre. Follow-up process adopted to ensure training benefits maximised.

CAREER HISTORY
**Previous role:**

**Area Sales Manager, Blue Building Society,** Responsible for 16 managers, 135 staff. Report to the Area Sales Director.

**Regional Sales Manager, Green Bank,** Responsible for 8 managers, 4 direct sales.

**Regional Manager, Green Bank**

**Assistant Regional Manager, Green Bank**

**Branch Manager, Green Bank**

**Branch Manager, White Building Society**

**Junior Management/Senior Clerical**

PERSONAL DEVELOPMENT
Sundridge Park Management Centre: leadership skills development

Peters Management Consultants: sales management training

Ashridge Management College: extensive internal training covering a wide range of topics

ADDITIONAL INFORMATION
Married – 1 son (29), 2 grandchildren

Fellow Chartered Building Society Institute

School governor/chairman of charitable trust

Computer literate: all Microsoft Office Software packages

INTERESTS
Fine wine, cooking, horse riding, trying to keep fit

Note the absence of dates, which disguises a period of unemployment. Janine Parks' functional CV disguises the fact that she was made redundant six months ago. This is not a 'definitive' CV, but is a real person's CV that has been adapted. It succeeded in getting an interview and securing a job.

A functional CV can really highlight your skills and attributes; but some recruiters are very wary of functional CVs. This is because they know that candidates may use this method to hide dark aspects of their past. That said, functional CVs can work and can win you an interview. Search Google for other examples of CVs – you'll find hundreds of examples, and then decide which style is best for you. Remember

> you can try different CVs with different employers to see if one works better than another

your CV isn't cast in stone or etched onto copper like printing plates used to be. You can try different CVs with different employers to see if one works better than another.

## Web-based, video and other CVs

So far we have concentrated on 'traditional' CVs, which can be posted on websites or e-mailed or mailed to employers. But the power of the internet doesn't stop there; indeed the way you present your CV using the latest websites and software is bounded only by your imagination.

We'll look at some of the options available, but for all of them the principles remain the same as in a traditional CV: the information must be up to date, relevant and well presented.

### Visual CV    www.visualcv.com

This is a website that gives you the opportunity to produce a multimedia CV to give prospective employers a comprehensive picture of your achievements, through video, images, links and text.

### LinkedIn    www.LinkedIn.com

Strictly speaking, LinkedIn is a professional networking website, but it has a CV-builder that allows people, including recruiters, to see your skills and experience. You're missing a trick if you are job hunting and you haven't posted a CV on LinkedIn. See Chapter 2, networking, for more about LinkedIn.

### Innovate CV    www.innovatecv.com

Like Visual CV, Innovate CV gives you the opportunity to produce a multi-media CV. It has other advantages, such as being able to import your LinkedIn profile and being able to upload your video CV. It also has 'training videos' to help you to develop a video CV and can link to your Facebook profile.

### YouTube    www.youtube.com

YouTube isn't only for ripped-off music videos and funny clips! It gives you the opportunity to post a video CV for the entire world to see at no cost. A video CV gives you a way to showcase your abilities beyond the capabilities of a traditional paper or web-based CV. The video résumé allows prospective employers to see and hear applicants, and to see how applicants present themselves. If you go to YouTube and search for CV or résumé, you'll find lots of other peoples' on-line video CVs to use as examples.

## Top Tips for YouTube/Video CVs

1 **Keep it short.** 3–5 minutes is optimum. (Script about 750 words.) The shorter the better.

2 **Hook them.** Grab the viewer's attention in the first 10 seconds.

3 **Make it visible.** PC screens are small. Ensure that you and anything you show or demonstrate can be seen easily.

4 **Showcase yourself.** Poor video = poor candidate. Only produce one if you KNOW it's going to sell you to recruiters.

5 **Show that you're different.**

6 **Show that you're motivated.**

7 **Convince them that you can do the job.**

Modern technology, such as CGI and other special effects, means that people nowadays have high expectations when they watch TV or movies. I once produced a 'video CV' to support the previous edition of this book using a webcam and CGI animation package, which is available free at **www.fix8.com**. The jury is still out on whether it was a good idea; if you would like to have a look at the clip go to YouTube and search my username GetThatJob (all one word). I wouldn't advocate the use of this method if you are applying for a job as a financial controller in a Fortune 500 company, but if you're applying for a job as a children's entertainer, it might be the one thing that differentiates you from the pack! Only produce a video CV if you are convinced that it's going to advance your success as a candidate. On the positive side, however, a short, well-produced, sincere and genuine video CV might be what puts you ahead of the pack and helps you to win the job offer!

*Slideshare*      **www.slideshare.net**
Slideshare is a good alternative to a video CV. With Slideshare you can produce a slideshow commercial of your CV in Microsoft PowerPoint and then share it with the world. For tips on using PowerPoint see Chapter 11. As with YouTube, there are lots of CVs already uploaded on **www.slideshare.net** to give you inspiration.

## Which CV is right for me?

The answer is the CV that gets you an interview for a job! They all have their pros and cons. A written CV, whether chronological or functional, is an essential starting point, but I would give serious consideration to adding web-based CVs and maybe, if appropriate, even a video CV to your inventory.

| CV type | Advantages | Disadvantages |
|---|---|---|
| **Written chronological** | • 'The Standard' must-have on which all other CVs are based<br>• Will appeal to' 'traditional' employers<br>• Essential for uploading onto recruitment websites | • Looks poor if too long or badly produced<br>• May be seen as too traditional/boring |
| **Written functional** | • All of the above<br>• Can hide periods of unemployment/sickness absence<br>• Can be used to hide your age | • All of the above<br>• Recruiters may be suspicious and think you have something to hide |
| **Web-based: Innovate, Visual and LinkedIn** | • Can be very professional-looking<br>• Worldwide reach for people searching for your skills<br>• Seen as 'honest' since you are opening your CV to the world<br>• Easy for people to forward recommend | • Public – anyone with internet access can see it<br>• Could be 'cloned'<br>• May be seen by your employer<br>• May be difficult to pull off sites once uploaded |
| **Video** | • Can look very slick and professional<br>• Relatively easy to produce and upload<br>• Recruiters get an insight into your personality and gravitas<br>• Can differentiate you from the rest | • Creates poor impression if poorly produced<br>• May be difficult to pull off sites once uploaded |

| CV type | Advantages | Disadvantages |
|---------|-----------|---------------|
| Slideshare | <ul><li>Can look very slick and professional</li><li>Can differentiate you from the rest</li><li>A 'big bang' for zero bucks: looks very good but free to use</li><li>Can differentiate you from the rest</li></ul> | <ul><li>Creates poor impression if poorly produced</li><li>May be difficult to pull off sites once uploaded</li></ul> |

## Message and medium

Whichever ways you choose to present your CV, remember the best CVs are the ones that have the correct balance of message and medium. The information must always be up to date, relevant and well presented.

# Chapter 5

## How to complete application forms and on-line applications

W hat an imposition – you spend all that time writing your CV, spot an ad in the newspaper for a job that sounds perfect and you ring to ask for details. They send you an information pack and an application form. Why should you now waste time completing an application form?

There may be a temptation to fill in your name and address at the top of the application form and write 'please see attached CV', then ping your reply in an e-mail. BUT DON'T – you might get away with it, but you almost certainly won't!

Organisations use application forms for two main reasons.

- To collect 'standard information' on all candidates, so that the person doing the initial screening can easily compare candidates against each other and against the job.

- So that candidates are 'forced' to provide important information. For example, a CV may simply state 'full driving licence', whereas the response to the application question 'Give details of any driving licence endorsements' may reveal '9 penalty points; 3 × speeding'.

Looked at from one viewpoint, an application form is a chore; from a positive viewpoint, it is your perfectly targeted CV!

# How to complete application forms

Virtually all application forms are completed on-line nowadays, but whether it's an on-line or a handwritten application, most of the principles are the same. First we'll concentrate on on-line applications.

- Read the form through before writing anything.

- Save a copy of the blank form and use it to draft your answers.

- Many applications have a word-count limit for different sections to force the applicant to be concise. Use the word count facility to keep checking and be ruthless – it's amazing what you can edit out of documents and still retain the meaning.

- Complete the form as requested. Stick to the font provided.

- If you need to expand any of the sections onto extra pages, type your name and the job applied for at the top of each page.

- Match your application to the job – review the job advertisement and any information you have received, such as the person specification or the job description, and match your application to the job. Draw up a checklist of their key requirements and, as you complete the application, make sure that you can give an example of how your skills, knowledge and experience match each of the criteria (see benefit statements in Chapter 6).

- Answer all the questions.

- Explain any gaps in your career.

- Maximise the 'Other information' opportunity by making a positive 'you' statement.

- Use feature and benefit statements to relate your past experience to the skills and qualities they are looking for.

- Don't include *any* negatives about yourself – this is not the place to be self-effacing.

- Telephone referees before putting them on the application. First as a courtesy, but second to help them to help you by bringing out your best points when they give a reference. You want them to emphasise your particular skills that are most relevant to the job.

- Proofread, proofread, proofread – and get someone else to do it.

- Keep a copy of the completed application – so that you know what you've said when you are invited for interview, and to add to your brag box! And also to use as a template for completing future applications. The power of copy and paste!

- Read the advertisement and try to second-guess any special requirements or words that they'll be looking for. There's a very good chance that your application will be scanned by dedicated software, programmed to look for keywords, and will reject your application if they aren't there.

- When you're completely satisfied that you have got it right, and have checked your spellings for the last time, go back on-line and copy and paste your text into their application form.

- Do a final check and click 'submit application'. You'll probably get an e-mail acknowledgement almost instantly. Don't get too excited – the software's programmed to do that as well. Good luck!

## How to prepare written applications

If you have been asked to submit an application through the post or write a hand-written application, then there's probably a good reason for it. It may be that the organisation is too small to be geared-up to receiving electronic applications, or it may be to see 'how you present yourself on paper'. For example, some organisations may ask for a printed application form accompanied by a handwritten letter of application.

- Complete the form exactly as requested. Black ink and block capitals doesn't mean blue ink (no matter how dark) and hieroglyphics!

- Use plain, white, quality paper.

- Use first-class postage or, if the organisation is local, make an opportunity to 'be in the area' and deliver it by hand (in the same clothes that you would wear for an interview). You never know, you might even get a chance to meet the recruiter, or at least his or her secretary – an opportunity to make a positive impression, distinguish yourself from the competition and increase the memorability of your application!

- If the application form is bulky, then double check that there's enough postage on the envelope. I once heard a sad story of a very senior local government official who was 'invited' to apply for a position. (In other words the job's yours but we've got to go through the formalities of advertising and interviewing!) The candidate spent a weekend completing the lengthy application form, posted it off in plenty of time and waited to hear. The deadline came and went and, as the interview date got nearer, he waited for his interview invitation. It didn't arrive. He rang and was told they had never received his application. A couple of days later, the applicant received the application pack that he had posted, endorsed 'Return to sender – DNA' (delivery not accepted). The clerk in the post room had refused to accept the package because there was a postage surcharge. The moral is obvious – check! If you want to be doubly sure and impress, use Special Delivery or, for a top job, why not use a courier service such as UPS or DHL?

# On-line applications: test drive the testing!

Recruiters will hate me for suggesting this, but why not try a few jobs that you wouldn't dream of really applying for as practice, before you start applying for real? It doesn't cost anything and all you'll lose is the time it took you to complete the form! Also, remember that when you do 'go live', the process will take a number of stages, and will also require you to check a number of times and then to confirm before you click 'submit'.

# Chapter 6

## How to sell yourself

What has selling got to do with getting a job? I'm a teacher, nurse, accountant, van driver ... Well, whatever job you want, while you are actively job hunting you are constantly selling yourself, whether by letter, telephone, e-mail or interview.

Every phone call is a sales pitch, every CV and job application is a sales brochure and every job interview is a sales call. And the product you are selling? Well, you.

Contrary to what you might think, 'selling' isn't only about charm, a smile and a pleasant personality. These are part of it but the selling process goes far beyond. There are many different techniques that are used by sales people to help customers to buy, and I believe that the most important one is presenting benefits.

> 'selling' isn't only about charm, a smile and a pleasant personality

## The importance of benefits

People buy things not for what they are, but for what they can do for them: make them look good, save them money, make them healthier, etc.

In the same way, organisations recruit people not for who or what they are, or for what they have done, but for what they bring to the company and what they can do for them.

# How to identify benefits

The process of identifying benefits is one that many people find difficult, so let's have a look at what's involved.

## What's the benefit of benefits?

I bought a mower with a 42-inch cutter deck because it meant that I wouldn't have to waste too much time cutting the grass. BENEFIT – I can do other things that I enjoy doing!

I bought an answerphone with a remote interrogation facility, so that when I stay away from home I can still keep in touch with my business contacts. BENEFIT – I keep in touch and don't miss out on business opportunities.

Benefit statements turn your gobbledygook into language that the other person can understand and is relevant to them. By using benefit statements you will help the recruiter to understand any technical jargon you may be using and help them to see the relevance of what you've done before the job you're being interviewed for.

Remember, in recruitment the recruiter is a 'customer' who is deciding whether to 'buy' your service for their company.

| Feature | Benefit |
| --- | --- |
| A description of product or service | Answers 'what's in it for me?' |
| A fact or characteristic | Answers what the features and advantages will ultimately mean to the user |
| A property or attribute of a product or service | Gives the value of worth that the buyer will get from the product or service |
| 'Because (of)…' | 'Which means that …' |

The following exercises will help you to develop benefit statements for yourself.

## How to identify benefits for a product/service

Imagine you're selling your used hatchback car. One of the features you might mention is its large boot. If you focus only on the feature, you would say, 'This car has a large boot.' But if you can turn that feature into a benefit by saying, 'The boot is large, which means that you can get three suitcases and your golf bag in there for a weekend away and still have plenty of room for any souvenirs you may buy', this makes a more powerful impression. The potential buyer can visualise how packing the boot for the next weekend away will be much easier.

Choose something that you have bought or sold recently. Write down two features in the 'Feature' column below. Now try turning each feature into a benefit (one feature can often give rise to a large number of benefits).

| Feature: what it is or has | Benefit |
|---|---|
| 'Because (of) …' | 'Which means that …' |

## How to identify benefits for you

People sometimes struggle when they are thinking about benefit statements for themselves, so, to inspire you, here's a feature benefit analysis for a candidate for an administrator job. As you can see, some of the features have produced a number of benefits.

| Feature: What have I done? What are my achievements? | Benefit: What it means to a prospective employer |
|---|---|
| 10 years of experience | • I have a good understanding of the expectations and requirements of the job. |
| | • I'm familiar with the duties that I'll be expected to carry out, as I have done similar work before. |
| | • I will only need a minimal amount of training or supervision. |
| | • Once I have completed my induction I'll be productive very quickly. |
| Typing speed 90 words per minute | • I can produce a 10-page report in less than an hour. |
| | • I can help you to increase your work output and meet and beat deadlines. |
| Excellent organiser | • I can organise your schedule so you'll always be on time and have the materials you need. |
| | • I can quickly retrieve any document or resource. |
| | • I prioritise my work to ensure the urgent projects are done first. |
| Loyal | • I support the company's overall mission and do whatever I can to help achieve it. |
| | • I don't complain about hard work or long hours. |
| | • I always work to the best of my ability. |

Identify four of your achievements that you are proud of and write them in the 'Feature' column. Convert your features to advantages and benefits for your target job.

| Feature: What have I done? What are my achievements? | Benefit: What it means to a prospective employer |
|---|---|
| 'Because (of) …' | 'Which means that …' |
| | |
| | |
| | |

At the end of each statement ask yourself 'So what?', to challenge the relevance of what you say to the recruiter. It may sound at first as if this process is mechanical and pointless, but it isn't – every time you develop a benefit statement for yourself, you are putting yourself in the recruiter's shoes. These benefit statements are extremely useful for building your CV, completing application forms and winning in interviews.

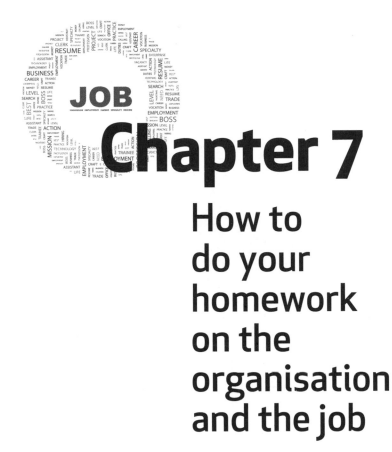

# Chapter 7

## How to do your homework on the organisation and the job

F ind out what you can about the job, the organisation, its products or services. There are two main reasons for doing this. First, the organisation will expect you to know what kind of organisation you'd be joining and also know something about their products or services. They want to know that you have a genuine interest in them and also that you're prepared to do some work! Second, your research should confirm to you what a good organisation you'd be joining and increase your motivation and interest in the job (or, conversely, you may discover something about the organisation that puts you off and makes you decide that you don't want to progress with your application).

## How to do your homework on the organisation

- Visit the organisation's website and search Google, or use one of the other search engines, to help you to find out more information. Don't be satisfied with just looking at the organisation's website, look at what other websites say about the organisation: have they received any awards recently; do they rank as one of the nation's best employers; have they recently introduced leading-edge products; what's their stance on recycling and reducing their carbon footprint; are they expanding or contracting; have there been any redundancies recently, etc. All of these questions and more will be answered when you use a search engine. An excellent website for researching companies is **www.kompass.com**. Get a copy of the annual report (if it's a plc or public sector organisation, they have to provide an annual report when requested) – you should be able to download one from their website. Phone the public relations or communications department, or go there in person. Get hold of product literature – getting a youngster to telephone the public relations department for a 'school project' is a good technique if you feel uncomfortable asking (although most people will view it positively if you request additional information). Research into the type of company – public, private, family-owned – and its performance compared with competitors, etc. Frankly, in today's information-rich environment, you may as well not bother turning up for the interview if you haven't done some basic research on the internet. Then you need to think about going the extra mile so that you can distinguish yourself from the rest of the pack!

● If you can, talk to people who use the organisation's products or services. A friend of mine, Michael, lost his job as a pharmaceutical salesman. He applied for a job selling replacement heart valves. Michael had no experience of selling surgical implants, so he went to the cardiac theatre at a large London teaching hospital and spoke to some of the surgical team about their use of replacement heart valves. A couple of days later he spent a whole day in an operating theatre seeing the products in use – and all he did was to ask the surgeon whether he could. And yes, he got the job! Now he's the company's managing director in Australia!

● Ask for a copy of the job description if one hasn't been supplied with the application information. (A job description is a document that clearly states what your duties will be, your decision-making latitude and how you will be assessed in the job-performance indicators.) If there isn't a job description, ask yourself why not? There may be a perfectly good reason, or it may be that they haven't yet decided what your duties will be (a potential source of discontent for the future). Don't view the absence of a job description necessarily as a negative; it may well be that the organisation has an informal structure and culture, and your job description may simply be 'whatever is needed to get the job done'. This kind of approach is particularly prevalent in creative, high-tech organisations that are about 'discovering and inventing the future'. NB: An employer doesn't have to provide a **detailed** job description, but there is a requirement to issue a statement of main terms and conditions of employment within two months of starting a job or any major changes to employment circumstances. One of the items of information that must be provided in this statement is an outline of the main duties of the employee.

- Re-read the advertisement, the application form (you did remember to keep a copy of it before you sent it?) and your CV. Highlight what you can offer to match their requirements. Bear in mind that when organisations recruit they rarely get a 'hand-in-glove' fit matching their requirements exactly. Your aim is to convince them that you are the *best* match.

## How to do your homework on the job

Present yourself well in an interview and you're probably 95 per cent of the way to getting the job. So it's useful to have some insight into how recruiters go about selecting candidates before you go to your interview. Many take a 'hit and miss' approach, with little structure. Good recruiters, however, work to a plan and set standards and requirements relating to a variety of factors. They then decide whether these are essential or desirable. This is known as a 'person profile' and is the recruiter's 'wish-list' for the ideal recruit.

present yourself well in an interview and you're probably 95 per cent of the way to getting the job

A recruiter will use the 'person profile' like a shopping list to try to help them to identify what the *ideal* candidate should be like. This may seem a little clinical but, if you think about it, it's no different to you sitting down and drawing up a list of criteria for a new family car:

- Must have manual gearbox.

- Must have five seats minimum, seven would be ideal.

- Prefer aircon, but sunroof is OK.

- Must be diesel.

- Prefer blue or grey metallic – definitely no bright garish colours!

- Prefer mileage below 25,000 but up to 60,000 OK if it has full main-dealer service history.

And so it goes on. You can then browse the internet, or visit the dealers with your checklist.

It's just the same in recruitment. For example, someone selecting a marketing executive might decide that it is essential that the person should be of graduate level and desirable that they should have an upper second-class honours degree. They may decide that it is essential that the person has very good interpersonal skills since they will be working with a variety of people. Some information is easy to establish (such as exam grades), while other information (such as interpersonal skills) involves judgement and evaluation of answers given to questions.

The person profile is the recruiter's shopping list to help them to identify the ideal candidate. The person specification must only include selection criteria that are legal. For example, it is illegal to discriminate as far as age is concerned in the UK, so a recruiter couldn't specify an ideal age for the worker. Below you will see a person specification for a job in a school as a Specialist IT Teaching Assistant. As you can see, many factors are essential *must haves* and you won't be considered if you don't have them, whereas others are desirable *nice to haves*. Some person specifications also include an extra column, to show how they will 'test' for the desired quality, whether by application form, interview, assessment test, or reference, etc. Many recruiters nowadays supply a job description *and* a person specification along with the application form as part of their application pack, and many even post these on the internet with the job advert. If there isn't a person specification, ask for a copy. If they haven't drawn up a person specification then search the internet for person specifications for similar jobs. But be cautious. Just as your requirements for a family car may differ from those of your neighbours, jobs with the same title will have different requirements in different organisations. When you are applying for jobs, work out who would be your 'ideal candidate' for the job if you were recruiting. What would you be looking for? Use the 'person profile' as a checklist and do what you can to show that you are the best match, and the ideal candidate.

## Nosuch Academy
## Person Specification for Specialist Teaching Assistant for ICT

| Requirements | Essential | Desirable |
| --- | :---: | :---: |
| ITQ ICT qualification, or equivalent at level 2 | ✓ | |
| ITQ ICT qualification or equivalent at level 3 or above | | ✓ |
| GCSE level 2 or above in English & Maths | ✓ | |
| Recognised Teaching Assistant Qualification | ✓ | |
| Enhanced CRB check | ✓ | |
| Certificate in Support/Learning | | ✓ |
| Ability to use Microsoft Word, Excel, PowerPoint | ✓ | |
| Ability to use Dreamweaver and Photoshop software | | ✓ |
| Knowledge of current developments in educational hardware and software | ✓ | |
| Experience of editing video, audio and photographic materials | | ✓ |
| Experience uploading materials onto existing websites | ✓ | |
| Recent (past 12 months) experience working with children or young people in a teaching & learning environment | ✓ | |
| Informed on issues of safeguarding young people's welfare | ✓ | |
| Discretion in everyday working life and in particular in dealing with confidential pupil information | ✓ | |
| Patience, and a positive attitude to interacting with pupils | ✓ | |
| Punctual, reliable and trustworthy | ✓ | |
| Ability to work both under teacher direction and, where appropriate, at own initiative in the classroom | ✓ | |
| Highly organised, self-motivated and able to organise own time as required when performing non-class-based duties | ✓ | |
| Clear communicator, both verbally and in writing | ✓ | |
| Willing to participate in full range of curriculum activities | ✓ | |
| Team worker with ability to contribute own ideas and to compromise when appropriate | ✓ | |
| Willing to undertake training and other CPD activities in order to further develop the specialist skills needed for the role | ✓ | |

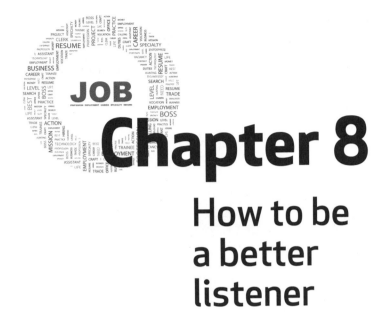

# Chapter 8

# How to be a better listener

Most of us are poor listeners ... 'Sorry, did you say something?' I said, most of us are poor listeners! We are so concerned with what we are going to ask or say that we ignore or miss a lot of what the other person says. I suspect that many of the people who read this book will have received some guidelines, training or coaching in 'talking to groups' at some time in their career. You wouldn't be reading this if your teachers hadn't taught you how to read and write. But I wonder how many readers have been trained in listening skills – even though it's the communication skill that you use more than any other.

> listening is the communication skill that you use more than any other

Improving your active listening skills will help you to collect valuable information in your research interviews, when you're networking and when you are being interviewed for a job. Active listening isn't easy. As a starting point you can improve your active listening by structuring your meetings and interviews as follows.

## Stages in a networking interview

1 Establish a relationship.
2 Encourage the other person to talk.
3 Reflect what the other person has said.

4   Summarise the key ideas you have got from the meeting.

5   Thank them for their time.

Look at the ten commandments of active listening, below. How many 'sins' did you commit in your last networking interview?

## The ten commandments of active listening

1   **Judgement evaluation** – do not judge or evaluate until you have understood!

2   **Avoid embellishment** – do not infer thoughts, facts or ideas in addition to those stated; avoid embellishment!

3   **Personal thoughts** – do not attribute your own thoughts and ideas to the speaker!

4   **Lack of attention** – do not allow your thoughts to stray nor your attention to wander!

5   **Attitude** – be receptive; do not close your mind to others!

6   **Wishful hearing** – do not permit your heart to rule your mind!

7   **Semantics** – do not interpret words and phrases except as they are interpreted by the speaker!

8   **Excessive talking** – do not become infatuated with the sound of your own voice!

9   **Lack of humility** – do not consider yourself too good to learn from any person!

10  **Fear** – do not fear improvement, correction or change!

# How to improve your listening skills

Simple techniques such as holding eye contact or nodding can improve your active listening skills.

| Non-verbal listening skills | Verbal listening skills |
|---|---|
| Show that you are listening actively and paying full attention by:<br><br>• Looking at the person.<br>• Nodding your head.<br>• Facial expressions, for example raised eyebrows or a smile.<br>• Attentive body posture, for example sitting forward. | Show that you are interested in what the other person has to say by:<br><br>• Rephrasing in your own words, for example 'So what you are saying is …'<br>• Summarising key points.<br>• Encouraging the other person to continue, for example 'That's interesting, tell me more.'<br>• Asking questions for further information or clarification, for example:<br><br>Why do you say that?<br>Why is that important to you?<br>What do you mean by that?<br>What does that mean to you?<br>Would you explain that further?<br>How does that relate to what you said before?<br>How did you do that?<br>When will the project be completed? |

One of the most powerful techniques for encouraging active listening is your use of open questions. Rudyard Kipling's reply when he was asked how he came to develop such a wide knowledge was:

*I keep six honest serving men*
*(they taught me all I knew);*
*Their names are What and Why and When*
*And How and Where and Who.*

You can't answer yes or no to questions that include: What, Why, When, How, Where and Who. They are excellent for gathering information and showing the other person that you are interested in them. One word of caution, beware of over-using 'why' as it can feel like an interrogation if it's repeated too many times. Examples of open questions are shown in the above table.

## Attitude

The chief requirement for active listening is to have 'room' for others – if you are preoccupied with your own thoughts, ideas and views, you are not mentally 'available' to listen effectively. When listening, it is really helpful to try to understand the other person's view, without superimposing your own views or judgements prematurely – a major block to active listening. Back to 'the ten commandments of active listening'!

> the chief requirement for active listening is to have 'room' for others

## Increase your odds to 2:1

In a nutshell, you'll improve your active listening if you ask more questions and you stop talking and start listening. You have two ears and one mouth. If you aim to use them in that ratio during your interviews and meetings (listen twice as much as you talk) you won't go too far wrong!

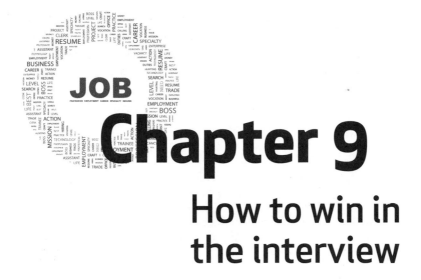

# Chapter 9

## How to win in the interview

The FBI says 'proper preparation and practice prevent a poor performance'. Prepare carefully and practise thoroughly before your interview. You will increase your confidence and your chances. Don't rely on charm and wit, there's too much at stake. Interviewers like well-prepared candidates who show a genuine interest.

Are you up to date with developments in your field? Scan the trade journals and the internet. What are the four or five latest innovations/initiatives/developments/trends? What are your opinions of them? You don't have to be a guru to be informed.

Read the day's local newspaper and a national paper, and scan any articles that might be directly related to the organisation. Also make a mental note of the main news stories of the day and formulate a view or opinion.

If you can, find out who will be interviewing you – think about what they might be looking for. This is particularly important if you are applying for a promotion or you already know the organisation well.

Decide an acceptable financial package – but let the interviewer raise it.

Plan your journey. There is virtually no excuse for being late for an interview. Allow extra time for rush-hour traffic, road works and finding a parking space.

# How to prepare for the interview day

Dress smartly in well-pressed, comfortable clothes appropriate to the job/organisation. Get your hair trimmed. Do what you can to make yourself feel good – if you feel good inside, you'll present yourself well on the outside.

Arrive early so that you can prepare yourself. Admiral Horatio Nelson is reputed to have said, 'I owe my success in life to always being 15 minutes before my time.' I can't vouch for the accuracy of the statement, but the principle is sound! Don't arrive more than 15 minutes before the interview, however – and wait outside. Some people view arriving much too early as poor time-management. They may be embarrassed to keep you waiting for a long time.

When you speak with receptionists and secretaries, remember they may be asked for their comments, as may the person who gave you an 'informal' tour of the site or offices before the interview.

Look around – could you work in these conditions, do people seem comfortable talking to each other, what is your impression of the culture? If you prefer a formal working environment where everyone is Mr or Ms, etc. and you hear first names being used the culture may not be right for you, and vice versa.

Leave the raincoat and umbrella in reception, so that you'll arrive at the interview uncluttered.

# How to conduct yourself in the interview

Smile and shake hands firmly, if the interviewer offers a hand. Wait to be invited to sit down. If the wait seems too long ask, 'Where would you like me to sit?'

If you're offered a drink, accept it. Even if you only take one or two sips, it will be very useful if your throat starts to dry up.

Remember, you are well on the way to a job offer. The interviewer hopes you're the right person! Take a few deep breaths, relax and be natural. This is your opportunity to show that you are the person they're looking for.

Sit well back into your chair, in an upright but comfortable position. If you use your hands when talking be aware of it and don't overdo it. Make friendly eye contact with the person asking questions. Don't stare. If you feel uncomfortable holding eye contact with people, look at the point of their forehead just above the nose – it works, honestly. If there is more than one interviewer, make sure you also involve them by addressing part of your answer to them. For panel interviews address the main body of an answer to the questioner, but then hold eye contact with other panel members in order to involve them. Only use the interviewer's first name if invited.

Brevity is the essence of good communication. Pause briefly for a second to think before you speak. Don't ramble, wasting valuable time. The interviewer is more interested in the quality of your answer than the quantity! Don't waste too much time talking about your early career; your recent achievements are usually far more relevant.

> brevity is the essence of good communication

Listen actively to what is being asked or said – if you need to get a better understanding, repeat or rephrase their question.

Be prepared for questions the interviewer knows you'll find difficult to answer, such as ones about a controversial subject. These are asked to see how you respond under pressure. Don't blurt out the answer – a short pause shows thoughtfulness.

Stress what it is about your skills and achievements that make you the person for the job. Introduce those five or six key 'You' points using benefit statements. Help the interviewer to see how your skills and experience will benefit their organisation. It will be too late if you remember when you're halfway home!

If the interviewer is your potential manager, ask yourself whether you will be able to work with him or her.

Have a notepad and pen handy in your bag, pocket or briefcase to take any notes and also to record the answers to your questions at the end of the interview. This shows you have thought about the job. Questions you might like to use are shown near the end of this section. Thank the interviewer and ask about the next step. This confirms your interest in the job.

Avoid:

- Criticising employers and recounting long stories about why you left jobs, particularly if you have a grievance with a previous employer.

- Talking about personal and domestic matters, unless asked.

- Getting on your soap box. What you do in your own time is of little concern to most employers, but few like activists or shop-floor politicians at work. Practise courteous answers to any likely questions.

- Mentioning salary/package. Let them know what you can do – this may well influence their view of what you are worth. Employers usually have a salary range in mind. If you ask about money too early they will give the lower figure. How many people do you know who have gone shopping to buy, say, a hi-fi system with a price in mind of £500–£650 only to find that they buy one for £725? The same happens in recruitment.

- Name-dropping. It can backfire!

- Interrupting the interviewer in your enthusiasm to make all your points.

● Pretending you've got a better offer elsewhere to try to push them into a decision. But do let them know if you're being interviewed by other people – it can sometimes focus their minds! They don't want to miss out on you, but don't give away too much information.

## How to prepare for their questions: 'Tell me about yourself' ... and others

You can't know what is going to be asked but you can improve your chances by practising some common questions – ideally with a friend. As I said earlier in the chapter, the most common question you are likely to face is *'Tell me about yourself'*. This is ranked as the interviewer's favourite question. If you answer it well you'll create a good first impression, which should put you in a positive frame of mind for the rest of the interview.

*Tell me about yourself:* I have asked it hundreds of times and received some excellent answers, but conversely I have had candidates who have missed the opportunity to sell themselves and said things like *'Well, there's not a lot to say'* or *'I've put everything in my CV.'* So prepare for this one well before the interview, by writing a short 'Me' statement. In one or two sentences **briefly** outline your personal circumstances: *'I'm married to Gill, we have two sons who are both at university and we live in Warminster.'* – The interviewer isn't interested in your collection of Beatles memorabilia, your passion for steam trains or your love of needlepoint! After the personal snapshot, make your first mini sales pitch: make five or six positive statements about yourself that focus on your work skills and achievements, rather than aspects at home. You might want to cover three major areas with examples of: your work ethic/approach to work; how you work with others; and finally your skills and achievements. Rehearse and commit the short statement to mind. When you're asked, try to sound as if you are speaking spontaneously rather than someone who has rehearsed. If you answer this question well you'll create a positive first impression with the interviewer and you'll boost your own confidence.

To prepare for this question, write five or six positive statements about yourself in the table below, remembering to include benefits (see Chapter 6). Focus especially on your work skills.

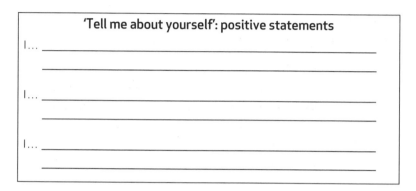

| 'Tell me about yourself': positive statements |
|---|
| I... _____ |
| _____ |
| I... _____ |
| _____ |
| I... _____ |
| _____ |

Now practise saying it – yes, I know it feels uncomfortable but it is worth it, because it does work.

Below I have listed some of the recruitment interviewer's favourite questions, with some guidelines on how you should answer them. As a set of general principles your answers should be honest and they should be framed to paint you in the best light by demonstrating your skills, knowledge, achievements and experience. Avoid giving answers that are self-effacing or that undersell you as a candidate. Also avoid any questions that might lead you to say anything that is less than complimentary about your previous employer, boss or colleagues.

Practise the interview with a friend who is prepared to give you some feedback. Use a tape recorder (your phone?), or better still a video camera to hear/see yourself as others do. Don't be despondent – we are all our own greatest critics and your accent isn't really that noticeable!

**Remember to keep your answers succinct!**

*Why did you leave your last job/why do you want to leave your current employer?*
No matter what the circumstances, don't be derogatory about previous or current managers, colleagues or the organisation. Say that you believe that you've realised your potential and are looking for a new opportunity or challenge.

*Are you successful?*
The answer has to be an unhesitant and unqualified: Yes. Then qualify the answer by giving a couple of examples from your personal life and three or four from your work life. Explain how you set goals for yourself and work towards achieving them. If you can't answer this question positively then you'll do yourself no good at all. Employers want to recruit winners not losers.

*What do your colleagues say about you?*
Be prepared with a quote or two from colleagues or your boss/ex-boss. Either a specific statement or a paraphrase will work well: *'My last boss used to say that I was one of the hardest workers she had ever known.'* I know the answer may make you blush, but interviews are no placc for modesty.

*What do you know about our organisation?*
If you've done your research then this should be easy. Focus on two or three positive things that you've learned about the organisation, which show why you are interested in working for them.

*What have you done to develop your skills/improve your knowledge in the past year?*
Focus mainly on activities that relate to the job. Organisations like to employ people who are flexible and keen to learn. If you can't answer this question, or your answer is *'nothing'*, you may be shooting yourself in the foot. A learning log is a good way to remember what you've learned over the year – why not put one together for the past 12 months?

*Are you a team player?*
Yes. Have two or three examples ready that show how you have contributed to the success of effective team-working in the past. Even lighthouse keepers have to work well with others, and team-working is a key element of many workplaces.

*Have you ever had to fire anyone? How did you feel about that?*
If you have fired someone then you'll probably agree that terminating someone's employment is one of the toughest situations that any manager has to encounter. On one hand you are taking away the employee's means of earning a living and depriving them of a good deal of dignity. On the other hand you are releasing your company from a contract with an employee who is failing to meet the required standards of working, or who is behaving in an unacceptable way. Be serious and factual in your answer and most of all keep the actual circumstances confidential. Talk about how you did what had to be done but took no pleasure in your responsibility.

*What would you bring to our organisation?*
You should be eager for this question. Summarise what you can bring to the organisation as well as what working for the organisation would do for your personal development. Don't be modest – this is the chance to 'sell' yourself.

*What are your greatest strengths?*
Don't be stuck for words. Be positive. Remember you were asked for your greatest strengths so choose about four. The following list might help: a good listener, a natural leader, a natural planner, a perfectionist, a team player, achiever, analytical, assertive, business-like, cautious, challenging, competitive, confident, conscientious, controlled, cooperative, decisive, deliberate, determined, direct, disciplined, exact, fast-paced, focused, friendly, goal-centred, helpful, independent, logical, non-aggressive, non-confrontational, opportunistic, organised, patient, personable, positive attitude, practical, quality focused, sensitive, straight-forward, structured,

supportive, task-oriented, trusting, understanding, you take the initiative. Recruitment definitely isn't an area where 'one size fits all'. Think about the job and then give the four or five strengths that you believe match what they are looking for.

*What would your previous boss say your greatest strength is?*
This is a variation on the last question. How about adding in a sprinkling of these: creativity, drive, energy, enthusiasm, expertise, hard worker, initiative, leadership, loyalty, patience, positive attitude, problem solver, team player, tenacity.

Remember the interview is a selling situation – you need to sell yourself positively (nobody else will) without being pompous or arrogant. Older candidates often undersell themselves, so focus on your answers to these two questions and think about examples from your past that demonstrate your personal qualities and skills.

> remember the interview is a selling situation

*What is your greatest weakness?*
Don't say that you haven't got any – we all have them and being able to recognise that shows a degree of self-awareness. That said, you do not have to 'confess your sins'.

If you say something such as, you get frustrated when you have to work with people who are prepared to accept low standards, people who only do just enough to get by or people who constantly criticise their employer, you'll effectively turn the question on its head. See also the next question.

*What kind of person would you refuse to work with?*
This is loaded to see if you are a team player and whether you get on with others. This time, instead of saying that you don't like shirkers or wingers, move to a higher ground and say that you'd have difficulty working with people who are disloyal to the organisation, violent people or people who discriminate against others.

*What motivates you to do your best at work?*
This will be entirely personal but might include things like: a challenge, achieving goals, being recognised, working for a fair boss, being stretched and learning new skills.

*Would you be willing to work overtime? Nights? Weekends?*
Be completely honest – there's no point saying you would just to get the job and then trying to re-negotiate when you start.

*Would you be willing to relocate if needed?*
You should obviously discuss this with your family prior to the interview, if you think there is a chance it may be asked. Answer honestly.

*Describe your leadership style.*
'*I've never really thought about it,*' or '*I just let people get on with it, and tell them to come to me if there's a problem*', just isn't good enough. If you're applying for a supervisory or managerial job that involves leading others you might need to learn a bit more about leadership styles. Search the internet for information on 'Situational Leadership' by Hersey and Blanchard, who advocate a flexible leadership approach that is appropriate to the situation and the follower's readiness.

*If you were recruiting a person for this job, what would you look for?*
Make sure that you mention skills and knowledge that are needed, and that you have!

*Don't you think you are overqualified/too experienced for this position?*
This is a common question for older candidates who have decided to apply for a job that is less senior/less responsible than their previous job. Talk about the challenges and the job satisfaction that you anticipate from a change of direction. Be positive and enthusiastic. The interviewer is probably concerned about a number of things: will the job be too boring for you or will you come in and start trying to change too many things? If the interviewer will be your new boss they might feel daunted because you

are more qualified and experienced than they are! Help them to feel comfortable with the situation.

*What qualities do you look for in a boss?*
You're on safe ground with something like, '*Someone who is skilled and knowledgeable, someone who has a good sense of humour, is fair and loyal to subordinates and someone who sets high standards.*' I don't think you'll find many bosses who don't think they have all of these traits.

*What is your work ethic?*
Stress how yours will benefit the organisation – determination, high standards and loyalty are a good start. What else would you add?

*What are your salary expectations?*
Never undersell yourself; be confident but not cocky. If you want to put the ball back in their court you could say something like '*I would hope to be paid a fair market rate, which takes account of my skills and experience. May I ask what that would be within your organisation?*'

> never undersell yourself

If you are still pressed for a figure then ask for an optimistic but rational figure. I know this may sound contradictory but what I mean is, if they have advertised a salary range and you're a brand spanking new trainee then it would be realistic to give a figure at or near the bottom of the range. If, however, you have lots of skills and experience then pitch somewhere between the mid-point and three-quarters of the way up the scale. And offer a rationale based on what you can bring to the job; show them that you will hit the ground running and that you'll be productive quickly. If they haven't advertised a salary range, then make sure that you have researched the market rate for the job on the internet and by looking at salary checkers, for example the one at Totaljobs: **www.totaljobs.com/salary-checker/salary-calculator**. See also Chapter 15 for advice on salary negotiation.

I could fill this book with suggested responses to questions but we would never cover every eventuality! Try answering some of the questions shown below. Paint the best image of yourself and show what you have to offer by talking about your skills and achievements.

Are you being interviewed for any other jobs?

Are you good at delegating tasks?

Are you seeking employment in an organisation of a particular size? Why?

Are you willing to travel for the job?

Can you explain this gap in your employment history?

Describe the best job you've ever had.

Describe the best boss you've ever had.

Describe the most rewarding experience of your career so far.

Do you have any hobbies? What do you do in your spare time?

Do you have plans for continued study? What are they?

Have you ever been dismissed (disciplined)? Tell me about it. (Tell them what you learned from the experience.)

Have you ever been fired or forced to resign?

Have you ever had difficulty with a supervisor? How did you resolve the conflict?

How are/were____ as employers?

How do you determine or evaluate success?

How do you plan to achieve your career goals?

How do you relax?

How do you spend your holidays?

How do you take direction?

How do you work under pressure?

How is your health?

How many days' sick leave have you taken in the last two years?

How well do you adapt to new situations?

How well do you work with people? Do you prefer working alone or in teams?

How would a good friend describe you?

How would you describe your career progress to date?

How would you evaluate your ability to deal with conflict?

In what kind of work environment are you most comfortable?

What are the qualities of a good leader?

What are the most important rewards you expect in your career?

What are the qualities needed in a good (job title)?

What are your expectations with regards to career development and salary increases?

What are your long-range and short-range goals and objectives?

What are your long-range career objectives?

What area of work do you feel least confident about?

What criteria are you using to evaluate the company for which you hope to work?

What did you enjoy doing at____?

What do you expect to be earning in five years?

What do you know about our competitors?

What do you really want to do in life?

What do you see yourself doing five years from now? Ten years from now?

What do you think it takes to be successful in a company like ours?

What have been your best achievements?

What have you accomplished that shows your initiative and willingness to work?

What have you been doing since you left____?

What have you learned from your mistakes?

What have you learned from your time with____?

What interests you about our products/services?

What major problem have you encountered and how did you deal with it?

What makes a good employer?

What makes you qualified for this position?

What motivates you to go the extra mile on a project or job?

What qualities do you look for when recruiting people into your team?

What two or three accomplishments have given you the most satisfaction? Why?

What two or three things are most important to you in your job?

What's more important to you – the work itself or how much you're paid for doing it?

What's the most recent book you've read?

What's one of the hardest decisions you've ever had to make?

Which is more important: creativity or efficiency? Why?

Why did you become a (job title)?

Why did you choose this career?

Why did you leave____?

Why should we offer you this job?

If you're asked to talk about your career history and you've had a variety of jobs, don't dwell on your early career – the interview will have been scheduled for a set time and it is usually more important to talk about current or most recent responsibilities and achievements.

## How to answer competency-based interview questions

A method of recruitment interviewing that is being used more and more by interviewers is called criteria-based, competency or behavioural interviewing. These are all different expressions for the same thing. The method attempts to take a more scientific approach to recruitment.

In the past, an interviewer may have asked a hypothetical question like, *'How would you react in ____ situation?'* For instance, *'What would you do if two of your sales representatives started a relationship?'* (I was asked that question once) or *'What would you do if you found that an employee had been fiddling their expense claims?'* In this situation the interviewee finds themselves 'second-guessing' the interviewer by saying what they think the interviewer wants to hear! It can become quite an amusing game!

Competency-based interviewing is far more scientific and is based on thorough research. Competence-based interviews are very structured and aim to assess your competence in the competency areas that the recruiter has identified are needed to do the job. The competency interview is based on three principles:

**Our past behaviour is a good predictor of our future behaviour.** Past performance is the best predictor of future behaviour; the way you have behaved in the past will give them the best indication of what you are likely to do in the future.

**Competencies are a good indicator of success at a job.** People who score highly on competencies during their interviews subsequently perform well in those competencies at work.

**Consistent structure.** By asking the same questions to each candidate the interviewer can compare responses and make a consistent comparison between them.

The interviewer will explore your competency in three broad areas, which are shown below.

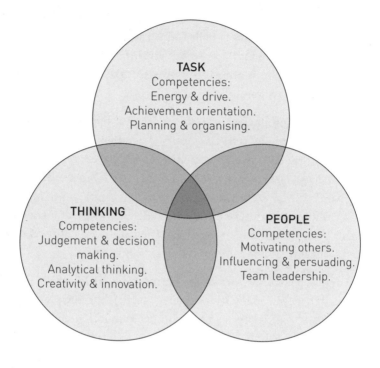

All jobs require elements from each of these three key areas. I can't think of a job that doesn't require an element of thinking, or an element of interacting with others. But all jobs will have a unique mix. For example, a job leading a team of 60 people will have a high 'People competencies' element, while a job as an accounts assistant will have a 'Task competencies' element.

What will happen before the interview is that the interviewer will review the competencies required for the job. These are listed in the person specification or in the job description, or in the job advert. Once they have identified the appropriate competencies they will choose questions to explore each of the competencies.

They will also use the same questions with each candidate. If there is more than one interviewer then they will probably divide the questions between the interviewers.

## How to handle competency-based interview questions

- Make each answer into a short story that has a beginning, a middle and an end.
- Help the interviewer to get a positive impression of you by:
  1 Describing the situation and what had to be done (beginning).
  2 Explaining what you did (middle).
  3 Describing the outcome in positive terms (end).
- The interviewer is looking for you to have handled situations in a positive way and for you to have learned from the experience. Make sure you show this in your answer.
- Keep your answers brief and to the point.

I was trained in behavioural interviewing skills over 20 years ago and I have used the method on many occasions. I have seen candidates shine in interview as they have answered questions competently. I have also seen candidates completely lost for words as they have fumbled mentally to compose an answer. Don't let it happen to you! Think about the competency-set that will be used in the job that you're applying for. Before the interview identify which competencies are needed for the job and practise answering the appropriate questions on the following pages. They seem simple, but they really are very searching!

**What they want to know: Are you adaptable/are you flexible?**

**What they will ask:**

- Tell me about a time when you changed your priorities to meet others' expectations.
- Describe a time when you altered your own behaviour to fit the situation.
- Tell me about a time when you had to change your point of view or your plans to take into account new information or changing priorities.

**What they want to know: Do you focus on clients'/customers' needs?**

**What they will ask:**

- Give an example of how you provided service to a client/stakeholder beyond their expectations. How did you identify the need? How did you respond?
- Tell me about a time when you had to deal with a client/stakeholder service issue.
- Describe a situation in which you acted as an advocate within your organisation for your stakeholder's needs when there was some organisational resistance to overcome.

**What they want to know: How well do you communicate with others?**

**What they will ask:**

- Describe a situation you were involved in that required a multi-dimensional communication strategy.
- Give an example of a difficult or sensitive situation that required extensive communication.
- Tell me about a time when you really had to pay attention to what someone else was saying, actively seeking to understand their message.

**What they want to know: How good are you at making decisions/ involving others?**

**What they will ask:**

- What are the most important decisions you have made in the last year? How did you make them? What alternatives did you consider?
- Describe an occasion when you involved others in your decision making. To what extent did you take note of their input?

**What they want to know: How do you develop others? (Essential for leadership/supervisory roles.)**

**What they will ask:**

- Tell me about a time when you coached someone to help them improve their skills or job performance. What did you do?
- Describe a time when you provided feedback to someone about their performance.
- Give me an example of a time when you recognised that a member of your team had a performance difficulty/deficiency. What did you do?

**What they want to know: Are you an achiever, or do you just put out enough to get by?**

**What they will ask:**

- Tell me about a project you initiated. What prompted you to begin it?
- Give an example of when you did more than was required.
- Give an example of when you worked the hardest and felt the greatest sense of achievement.

**What they want to know: Do you have good interpersonal skills? How well do you get on with others? Are you sensitive to differences in people?**

**What they will ask:**

- Describe a situation where you wished you'd acted differently with someone at work. What did you do? What happened?

- Can you describe a situation where you found yourself dealing with someone whom you felt was over-sensitive? How did you handle it?

- What unpopular decisions have you recently made? How did people respond? How did that make you feel?

- What are some of the most difficult one-to-one meetings you have had with colleagues? Why were they difficult?

**What they want to know: Are you innovative – do you come up with new ideas?**

**What they will ask:**

- Describe something you have done that was new and different for your organisation that improved performance and/or productivity.

- Tell me about a time when you identified a new, unusual or different approach for addressing a problem or task.

- Tell me about a recent problem in which old solutions wouldn't work. How did you solve the problem?

**What they want to know: Do you have an impact on others? Can you influence people?**

**What they will ask:**

- Describe a recent situation when you convinced someone or a group to do something.
- Describe a time when you went through a series of steps to influence either an individual or a group on an important issue.
- Describe a situation in which you were able to influence different stakeholders with differing perspectives.

**What they want to know: How well do you lead others?**

**What they will ask:**

- Tell me about a time when you had to lead a group to achieve an objective.
- Describe a situation where you had to ensure that your 'actions spoke louder than your words' to a team.
- Describe a situation where you inspired others to meet a common goal.
- Have you been a member of a group where two of the members did not work well together? What did you do to get them to do so?
- What do you do to set an example for others?

**What they want to know: Are you aware of 'the big picture'? Are you organisationally aware?**

**What they will ask:**

- Describe the culture of your organisation and give an example of how you work within this culture to achieve a goal.
- Describe the things you consider and the steps you take in assessing the viability of a new idea or initiative.
- Tell me about a time when you used your knowledge of the organisation to get what you needed.

**What they want to know: Are you organised? Do you plan well?**

**What they will ask:**

- What did you do to get ready for this interview?
- How do you decide priorities in planning your time? Give examples.
- What are your objectives for this year? What are you doing to achieve them? How are you progressing?

**What they want to know: Are you a good problem solver? Do you have good judgement?**

**What they will ask:**

- Tell me about a time when you had to identify the underlying causes of a problem.
- Describe a time when you had to analyse a problem and generate a solution.
- Tell me about a situation where you had to solve a problem or make a decision that required careful thought. What did you do?

**What they want to know: How well do you build working relationships?**

**What they will ask:**

- Describe a situation in which you developed an effective win/win relationship with a stakeholder or client. How did you go about building the relationship?
- Tell me about a time when you relied on a contact in your network to help you with a work-related task or problem.
- Give me an example of a time when you deliberately attempted to build rapport with a co-worker or customer.

**What they want to know: How well do you manage your resources?**

**What they will ask:**

- Describe a situation in which you took a creative approach to resourcing in order to achieve a goal.

- Tell me about a time when you had to deal with a particular resource-management issue regarding people, materials or assets.

- Describe the options you would consider to resource a project or goal if you did not have the available resources within your own span of control.

- Describe a situation in which you established a partnership with another organisation or stakeholder to achieve a mutual goal. What steps did you take to ensure the partnership was effective?

**What they want to know: Can you get results?**

**What they will ask:**

- Tell me about a time when you set and achieved a goal.

- Tell me about a time when you improved the way things typically were done on the job.

- Describe something you have done to improve the performance of your work unit.

- Describe something you have done to maximise or improve the use of resources beyond your own work unit to achieve improved results.

**What they want to know: How well can you sell your ideas?**

**What they will ask:**

- What are some of the best ideas you ever sold a superior/subordinate? What was your approach? Why did it succeed/fail?

- Describe your most satisfying (or disappointing) experience in attempting to gain support for an idea or proposal.

**What they want to know: Self-management – do you control your time or does it control you?**

**What they will ask:**

- Describe the level of stress in your current job and what you do to manage it.
- Describe a time when you were in a high-pressure situation.
- Describe a time when things didn't turn out as you had planned and you had to analyse the situation to address the issue.

**What they want to know: Do you think strategically?**

**What they will ask:**

- Describe a challenge or opportunity you identified based on your industry knowledge, and how you developed a strategy to respond to it.
- Describe a time when you created a strategy to achieve a longer-term business objective.
- Describe a time when you used your business knowledge to understand a specific business situation.

**What they want to know: Are you a team player? How well do you work alongside others?**

**What they will ask:**

- Tell me about a time when you worked successfully as a member of a team.
- Describe a situation where you were successful in getting people to work together effectively.
- Describe a situation in which you were a member (not the leader) of a team, and a conflict arose within the team. What did you do?
- How do you work as a team member? Give examples.

Of course, you won't be asked all of these competency-based questions; the interview would last forever! As I mentioned earlier, by identifying the competencies required for the job and practising the appropriate questions you really can improve your chances of succeeding at interview.

These questions can be intimidating, but they can also be an excellent opportunity for you to demonstrate that you are the candidate with the best competencies to do the job!

## How to handle illegal interview questions: discrimination

If you think about it, the recruitment process is a process of discrimination: all other thing being equal, the recruiter is more likely to select someone with a first-class honours degree than a third, or someone with five years' experience over a candidate with no experience, etc. The recruiter is discriminating between candidates to make the best choice.

But there are many factors that the recruiter cannot discriminate against. In addition to other laws, The Equality Act 2010 protects employees and applicants for employment against discrimination relating to certain 'protected characteristics'.

> there are many factors that the recruiter cannot discriminate against

These protected characteristics are:

- Age

- Disability

- Race (including ethnic or national origin, nationality and colour)

- Religion or belief

- Sex (including discrimination based on pregnancy or maternity leave)

● Sexual orientation

● Gender reassignment

This means that there are a lot of things that interviewers cannot ask you about during interview. If they do they are breaking the law. The following types of questions should not be asked by a recruiter during an interview (this includes recruitment agencies), and you have the right to decline to answer these if they are asked (we'll look at how to decline to answer at the end of this section):

## No-go areas for interview questions

● How old are you?

● Are you married?

● Are you gay?

● What are your childcare arrangements?

● Are you planning to start a family soon?

● Are you a member of a trade union?

● What political party do you support?

*Source: Which?* Magazine

**Not allowed:** *'How old are you?' 'How many more years do you plan to work before you retire?'*

**Age:** Age discrimination laws have changed a lot in recent years and you should not be asked questions about age in a job interview. In employment law, this is considered to be irrelevant to your ability to perform a specific role or task. An interviewer can, however, ask whether you are over 18 if it is a legal requirement of the job. If you have applied to be a barman or work in a casino, then an employer has a legal obligation to find out this information.

**Not allowed:** *'Do you take medications?' 'How tall are you?' 'How much do you weigh?' 'Do you have any disabilities?' 'Have you had any recent or past illnesses or operations?'*

**Disability and health**: Interviewers need to tread carefully. They can legitimately ask you to explain significant amounts of sickness absence. However, they cannot ask about a disability and whether or not that would affect your ability to do the job.

**Not allowed:** *'Are you a UK citizen?' 'What is your native tongue?' 'How long have you lived here?' 'What religion do you practice?' 'Do you belong to a club or social organisation?'*

**Place of birth, ethnicity and religion:** Employers *can* ask you at a job interview if you have the correct paperwork to legally work in the UK and they can ask you to provide evidence of this. The employer has a statutory obligation only to employ people who can legally work and they can be fined if you don't have the correct paperwork. They are not allowed, however, to probe into information about your place of birth, nationality, race or ethnic background. Employment law considers these factors to be irrelevant in the job selection process as they have no bearing on your ability to perform employment tasks. It is legal for information on ethnic background to be asked for on an equal opportunities form; the reason for this is strictly for monitoring purposes and is usually included as a separate attachment from the main application form. This information cannot be used as part of the selection process.

**Not allowed:** *'Is this your maiden name?' 'Do you plan to have children?' 'Do you have kids?' 'What does your dad do for a living?' 'We've always had a woman do this job. Do you think you will be able to cope as well as they did?' 'How do you feel about supervising a team of men?'*

**Marital status, children and sexual preference:** Interviewers should not ask questions about your marital status, children you may have or your sexual preference. All could be grounds for discrimination. The employer can, however, ask questions about whether there are any factors that would hinder your performance in certain jobs. If you have applied to be a sales rep, for example, an employer can ask whether there are factors that would restrict your ability to travel or spend time away from home, provided that this is a specific requirement of the job. They can ask this and only this; they can't go on to ask about childcare arrangements or how you will cope with looking after an elderly relative.

**Not allowed:** *'Do you smoke or drink?' 'Do you belong to a trade union?' How much do you weigh?'*

**Lifestyle choices:** It's also illegal to ask you questions relating to your personal lifestyle choices – for example, about your consumption of alcohol, whether you smoke or use recreational drugs. A company can set rules regarding the use of these kinds of substances and state what is and is not permitted at work, but what an employee does outside of work and work time is not the company's business and, therefore, they can't ask about these things at interview. You shouldn't be asked questions about membership or affiliations with any organisations, such as whether you are a member of a political party or a trade union. Questions about height and weight are also discriminatory unless the job is exempt in terms of it being necessary to have a certain minimum height requirement. For example, you can join the Territorial Army as a chef if you are 148cm tall or over, but you need to be a minimum of 158cm to be an ammunition technician.

**CRB checks:** For certain jobs employers are entitled to run a Criminal Records Bureau (CRB) check on you, either prior to interview or afterwards. (An enhanced CRB check costs just under £50 so many employers will interview you and then make a job offer subject to a satisfactory CRB check.) These are usually jobs that involve working with children, young people or vulnerable adults, or jobs that involve close contact with the public, such as taxi drivers. You'll either pass or fail the CRB check; the contents of the document aren't a topic of conversation for the interview. If you have a criminal record you'll find links to useful websites in Appendix 1 under 'Rehabilitation of offenders'.

**Miscellaneous questions that shouldn't be asked**: *'How far is your commute?' 'Do you live nearby?' 'Have you ever been arrested?' 'Were you honourably discharged from the military?' 'Are you a member of the Territorial Army/Special Constabulary/other volunteer force?'*

## How to reply to illegal interview questions

A recruiter who asks inappropriate questions is likely to be out of touch with modern employment laws, and the probable reason why they have asked the question is that they have not received sufficient training. I genuinely believe that the majority of 'illegal' questions are asked by accident, rather than design. If you are asked an illegal question then you still want to create a good impression and avoid confrontation, so my best advice is to say something like *'Oh, I didn't think you were allowed to ask that'* rather than *'You aren't allowed to ask that!'*

What happens next is entirely your decision; you may feel that although the question is illegal it's not intrusive and you may go on to say *'... but I don't mind answering it'* and proceed by answering the question. Alternatively, if you do not want to answer the question then *'I would prefer not to answer that question'* would be a perfectly reasonable thing to say. And then move on quickly. The interviewer will probably be embarrassed that they have asked the question!

## Taking it further

The laws on employment discrimination are very strong and, if you believe that you have been discriminated against during the selection process, you may wish to take it further. Compensation in these cases can be quite substantial if you can prove it. The internet is a rich source of advice on how to do this, but a starting point may be to go along to your local Citizen's Advice Bureau to discuss it with one of their advisors. Useful websites for ACAS and others can be found in Appendix 1 under Legal and general advice.

Author's note: The information given here is based on my knowledge and experience as a human resources professional and is up to date at the time of writing. The law is constantly changing. If you are considering legal proceedings then it is essential that you obtain legal advice from a qualified lawyer.

## How to prepare and ask your own questions

Your interview is a two-way process. If they offer you the job, you may be making a choice about where you will spend a significant part of your working life. Make the most of your opportunity to find out what you need to know and also to create a business-like impression. Start with questions that show an interest in the job, not what the company can do for you.

> your interview is a two-way process

Make a note of what you want to ask beforehand. When the interviewer asks if you have any questions, produce your notebook or notepad and take brief notes of the answers given. Don't think that the interviewer will think you're 'showing off' – quite the opposite. They'll be impressed that you have thought about the job and done some preparation. Examples of information you might like to gather (but not all at once!) are given below.

### Your questions about the job

- What will my daily responsibilities/duties be?

- What is the level of the job within the company's grading structure?

- To whom does the job report?

- Is there a job description/what are the main priorities?

- Reporting – up/down/sideways – are there any dotted-line responsibilities?

- What will be my budget availability?

- What will be my goals/targets/priorities?

- What are relationships like with other departments?

- What are the people like for whom I would be responsible?

- Are there any 'management' issues?

- In what way is the company committed to my training and development?

- What are the opportunities for progress/career advancement?

- What resources would I have available to help me achieve my goals?

## Your questions about the organisation

- What is the UK/total turnover?

- Is there a statement on company philosophy/mission statement?

- What is the company's profitability budget compared with competitors

- How big is the workforce/turnover (of staff)?

- What is the range of UK services/products?

- What is the company's e-commerce strategy?

- What new products/services are under development?

- What innovative ways are used to market products/services?

- Where will the organisation be in five/ten years?

## Your questions about the practical aspects

Questions for when you are on the home straight! You won't need to ask all of these questions since most of them will have been answered through the selection process.

- Medical – is it required?

- Start date – how soon?

- Pension – how is the scheme structured? Can you transfer in?

- Salary review – based on what? How often? When will your first one be?

- Car – allocation/running costs or charge?

- Average salary increase last year/previous years? How is it reviewed? Holidays?

- Private healthcare – is it available? How much does it cost? Is spouse/family covered?

- Insurance – what is the company scheme?

- Bonus scheme – what is the structure?

- Share options – are they available?

- Salary – where does the figure they have offered fit in on their salary scales? If they want to start you at the bottom of the scale, ask why and try to convince them that your experience/ skills justify being started higher on the scale.

## How to close the interview

your closing comments and questions and your body language are very important

What we say in the first two minutes of meeting people and what we say in the last two minutes has a large effect on the impact we make on them. Your closing comments and questions and your body language are very important if you want to leave a strong impact and set yourself apart from the competition.

The interviewer may well have covered some of the following points in their summary, but if they haven't here's a checklist:

- Tell the interviewer that you have enjoyed meeting them and learning more about their organisation.

- Re-confirm that you are interested in the position. Say that you hope that you will be chosen to progress to the next part of the selection process (if it's part of an ongoing process) or that you will be offered the job (if it's a final interview).

- Summarise and re-state five or six of your key skills that match the job. Unless you've learned something new about the job during the interview, these will be the same ones you used in your 'Tell me about yourself' positive statements at the start of the interview.

- Re-state any added value you can bring to the job – for example, if you are a business skills teacher but can offer IT or Maths as an additional subject.

- Ask if there is anything else they need to know about you or any information that they would like you to provide, such as references or copies of certificates.

- Ask them to tell you what the next step in the process will be.

- Ask when the decision will be made and how you will find out.

- Find out how to contact them and also whom you should contact if you need to get in touch after the interview.

These questions not only confirm that you are genuinely interested in the job, they also show that you have a thorough, business-like approach to your work.

Remember to shake hands, smile and thank everyone for their time and leave the meeting in a positive, up-beat way. Remember you're 'on parade' until you leave the building. If an interviewer or another member of staff takes you to reception, use the opportunity to tell them, in an informal way, just how impressed you are with the organisation and how much you would like to work there.

## After the interview

Relax and congratulate yourself on having been as well-prepared as you could have been. Reflect on how it went and write down key points that could be important in another interview.

You'll probably have to wait to hear the decision, but in the meantime you can learn from the experience.

- Were you happy with the way you handled yourself?
- Did you say what you wanted to say?
- Did you find out what you needed to know?
- How many of your 'you' points did you get across?
- Was your behaviour positive, assertive, humble, tense, laid-back, talkative, controlled, etc.?

If you were put forward by a recruitment agency, call them as soon as you can to let them know how you got on and to confirm your interest in the job. They will almost certainly feed this straight back to the interviewer and it will be positively viewed. Otherwise, leave the ball in the court of the interviewer. Don't become too despondent if you don't hear for a while – recruitment can sometimes take many weeks.

If, however, they have promised to let you know, one way or the other, by a certain date and that comes and goes, there is no harm done by telephoning to see how soon you are going to find out their decision.

Remember that the interviewer is hoping that you are the right person for the job, just as you are hoping to get the job. Do prepare and practise. It will be worth it.

the interviewer is hoping that you are the right person for the job

## Emerging technologies – interviews in the future (and now!)

The rate of change in modern technology means that some recruiters, like many other people, continue to explore new possibilities. A friend of mine from the UK was interviewed by webcam on the internet for a lecturing job in Australia. The images were a little jumpy but this was acceptable compared with the cost of flights (and she got the job!).

Video, on-line and telephone interviews are becoming more and more part of everyday recruitment practice, because of their convenience and cost-saving. *Don't be daunted* by the new technology! Remember, all these new methods used by recruiters are nothing more than tools to help them to make the best decision. They are not an end in themselves. And for the foreseeable future, I believe, interviews in person will continue to be our most popular selection method.

For more information on video interviews and other emerging technology have a look at: **new.hirevue.com/how-it-works/whomever** and also **www.jobs2web.com**. These websites are aimed at employers to encourage them to use their services, but it will give you some tips on what you will need to do to prepare if you are interviewed by webcam, blog, messenger or any of the other emerging technologies. You might also want to have a look at **jobsinpods.com**, an American website for recruiters that is encouraging employers to use iPod technology. I personally can't see the benefit and don't know of any UK recruiters using this method, but who knows what the future might bring?

Whatever selection methods you encounter, the most important thing to remember is that the recruiter is recruiting a person. Prepare and practise thoroughly. When you get to the selection process, let the power of your personality persuade them that you are the person they should recruit!

Good luck!

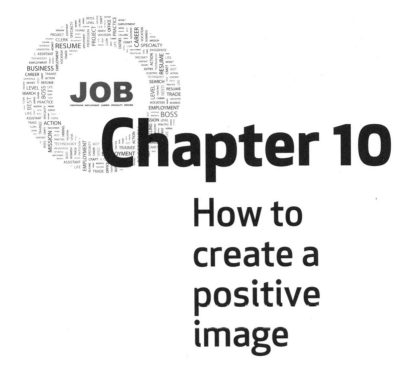

# Chapter 10

# How to create a positive image

B ack in the 1980s I used to work for a large American corporation. One of its subsidiary companies was a world-famous cosmetics company that produces a top-quality, top-selling face cream. At the time the cream sold for around £40 a pot; £40 was a lot of money in the 1980s! I was quite shocked when I attended a meeting where I found out about the manufacturing costs and discovered that the glass pot and the packaging cost three times more than the contents! But I shouldn't have been. You see, it was an excellent, top-quality product and the expensive pot, packaging and branding created a positive image for the product that made customers comfortable with the idea that they were buying a premium product. In just the same way you need to package yourself well and create a positive image so that the recruiter feels comfortable when they make the 'buying decision' to hire you.

In the CV and job application chapters we have looked at what you can do to package yourself well in writing, and later in this chapter we'll have a look at what you can do to present a positive image through appropriate dress and positive body language.

The first step to creating a positive image is to ensure that you don't create a negative image and commit 'candidate suicide'.

## How to avoid committing 'candidate catastrophes'

I sometimes feel that I'm being a little patronising when I stress things such as the importance of attention to detail when it comes to presenting yourself well as a candidate. The importance of neatness, thoroughness, tenacity, politeness and the multitude of other skills you need to use if you want to get that job should be second nature, shouldn't they? When I talk to people about candidates who have missed their chance through committing 'candidate catastrophes' there's often a feeling of *well it's obvious, isn't it?* and *nobody would do anything so stupid would they?* BUT throughout my career I've seen people who have committed 'candidate catastrophes' by making the silliest mistakes in their job applications, CVs and in interviews. For example, well-qualified applicants who make stupid typographical errors and go straight onto the 'regret' pile. Or people who copy and paste the content of a previous letter of application and forget to change the addressee's name! Or people who turn up for interviews dressed inappropriately. Or people who patronise the interviewer. Or people who apply on-line and forget to attach their CV – whoops!

I did an internet search to see if things had changed for the better, so that I could see whether I should stop beating my drum. Regrettably, I have to say that, if anything, things have got worse and applications have become sloppier – probably because electronic communication is so fast that many people fail to check things as thoroughly as they should. So, further on in the chapter I *will* beat my drum and talk about how you can succeed in the selection process.

Before that let's have a look at some examples of 'candidate catastrophes'. On first impression the examples are quite amusing, but they are all stories of disaster because every one of them represents a lost opportunity – a job application or interview that was unsuccessful because of an avoidable mistake that meant the candidate didn't get that job!

- The candidate who gave his e-mail address as LAZY_BOY@ domain.com. Lesson: if you use a fun e-mail address, or a family e-mail address such as thewaltonsfamily@ waltonsmountain.com, keep it for personal e-mails and register a new e-mail address for your job applications.

- Then Brian – who sent his CV out with his name spelled BrAIn and wondered why he'd had no responses to his applications in two months. Lesson: check, check and re-check. And take notice of the squiggly lines from your spell checker!

- The applicant whose cover letter said he was sending it to the HR Director, as a 'courtesy' before 'making any attempt to sidestep' their authority and going directly to the 'real decision maker' (who was the HR Director!). Lesson: there is no place for being smart in job applications.

- An electronic application that contained a hyperlink to the applicant's own website, with photographs of the applicant in a state of undress! Lesson: interesting viewing maybe, but not a way to create a good first impression.

- An applicant said their résumé was posted to a particular website from which the recruiter should download it. The recruiter didn't bother! Lesson: your job is to make things easy for the recruiter, not make work for them.

Many of the above examples came from around the world, and so to get a picture of UK recruitment I asked members of the Chartered Institute of Personnel and Development, Europe's largest institute for human resource professionals, for examples. Their examples of 'candidate catastrophes' are on the following pages; I have been assured that every one of these is a true story.

## Candidate catastrophes – interviews

- A candidate who arrived late and told me (without being asked) that his worst quality was his laziness.

- A woman who thought it was perfectly reasonable to answer her mobile in the middle of an interview.

- The woman who thought I was the (male) manager's secretary and was extremely rude and patronising to me. When she finally realised that I was the manager and the interviewer she acknowledged that it was unlikely she would get the job – she was right!

- In a recent interview for a Project Manager the candidate was asked which aspect of Project Management he didn't like and replied *'change'*! Quite worrying …

- The 16-year-old candidate who arrived with his mother. Without asking, she came into the interview and proceeded to answer every question on his behalf. I decided to ask the question: *'Have you experience of making decisions for yourself?'* His mother replied, *'Yes, he is very independent'*. Neither he (nor his mother) got the job.

- I was trying to arrange an interview with a candidate and we were finding it difficult to synchronise diaries. He said he would try and free up a particular day. He called me back and said *'Oh sod it, I will take the day off sick, I'll be leaving soon anyway.'*

- The candidate who turned up for a Database Developer role drunk, at 9:30 in the morning. Dutch courage is never the best way to deal with pre-interview nerves.

- The candidate for a Customer Contact Centre role who, when asked why she wanted the role, replied *'What role is this again? I have applied for so many.'*

- The candidate who drank so much water through nerves that he needed the toilet halfway through the interview.

- When asked *'How would you handle being asked to work on a project that you didn't personally like?'* the answer was *'I'd refuse to do any work.'*

- A candidate stopped me during a telephone interview in order to have a conversation with his flat mate.

- The candidate for a 100 per cent phone-based telesales role who admitted to not enjoying selling on the phone, or even talking to people on the phone.

- A colleague interviewed someone who turned up covered in blood … When asked if he was OK, he said '*Oh yes I'm fine, I just got into a fight on the way here*'!

- The manager who was interviewing with me asked the candidate about their interests and hobbies (her CV said she liked to watch Vietnamese films and was interested in weapons). She said, '*Oh I am extremely interested in and have over 50 old Vietnamese films; I think that they are true to life in the way they show the violence, torture and rape inflicted on women and children.*'

- A candidate made it clear from the start he had a problem with women, and I, a female, was the main interviewer! When I asked him a question, he replied to the man I was interviewing with.

- I interviewed someone for a job as a porter who was on his way home from Glastonbury festival, complete with mud, no shoes and vomit on his shirt.

- An applicant for a senior manager post, when asked how he would deal with a difficult staff member, said that he would dismiss them on the spot! Ouch!

- A candidate who was ten years my junior flirted his way through the interview … laughing, smiling, leaning over the table and stopping to tell me where he felt sore and finishing off by showing me his tongue piercing. He didn't get the job.

## Candidate catastrophes – applications

- I turned a candidate down at application stage recently; his father phoned the company to complain about me and sent an e-mail to the MD suggesting that the MD and I go to a family BBQ so we could see what a great guy his son was!

- We had an application by e-mail where HELLO was spelled out in the shape of jelly beans (we are quite a serious public sector international organisation).

- The candidate who claimed to have a 'City & Gills' didn't get an interview.

- The application form with a clipped wedding photograph where a passport photo was supposed to be, with arrows and a comment 'that's me!'

- A speculative application from a man looking for an admin position. He didn't put a stamp on the envelope so we had to pay £1.12 to receive it and the cover letter had numerous spelling and typing errors.

- An application for a job as a shop assistant in a major high street store that included details of their (still unspent) conviction for shop lifting.

- The man who had put one of his previous jobs as 'Fork Lift Truck Driver'. In the section entitled 'Reason for Leaving' he had put 'I lied about having a fork lift truck driving licence'!

- On an application form (pre-Equality Act, of course!), I once received the following response: Marital Status: *Average.*

- Our games company was recruiting sound designers. One applicant sent in a note torn from a notebook, written in pencil saying *'please find enclosed my CD – I hope we can make beautiful music together – lots of love* (yes he put that) *X'.* The CD was blank and he sent no contact details!

- An e-mail to apply for a role with us for 'digilal marketing' (I assume he meant digital ...). He attached his CV via a web link. The link, however, was to a 'CV-builder website homepage', and not his CV!

- In response to a question on the application form, *'What areas would you like support to improve in?'* one candidate responded, *'While there is always room for improve, i do not feel that I has any area in which i require imorpvmeent.'* (their spelling, not my poor typing!).

- A CV for a QC Technician. Under key skills they wrote: *'Attenshion to detail.'*

- A CV with the applicant's photograph at the top showing her in chains and hanging off a pole in 6" stilettos and a micro skirt – nice.

- Having worked for a well-known utility company about a decade ago that took on several apprentices every year, I am fairly used to fielding calls and letters from the disgruntled parents of 'poor Timmy' who only 'wants a job'.

- But fast-forward to my current job, we received a speculative application from a chap looking for work. He got turned down, politely, because we weren't looking for anyone at the time. His mum decided to write in. Not to me but to the MD. So far so normal. He was 46.

- Another candidate didn't turn up for interview. When we eventually got hold of him he said he had a bit of a cold and, anyway, he couldn't remember exactly when the interview was (he had my contact details, and the college had confirmed the time to him the day before) so he thought he'd wait for us to get in touch so that he could ask to reschedule ... funnily enough we declined to do so!

- An applicant's answer in the 'Health' section of an application form: *'My concise answer? I'm not too bad. My less concise answer? Since I am a man, and all men are mortal, it must therefore follow that I am mortal. So, it's not like I'm impervious to the ravages of disease and time. Or that no weapon or force can destroy me.'*

- A young man's response to 'SEX?' on the application form – a sheepish 'twice'.

Every one of these stories is an example of an avoidable 'candidate catastrophe' and every one represents a lost opportunity for someone to get a job. In spite of the recession and high unemployment there is a shortage of skills and employers are keen to employ talented people; but they aren't desperate. The general principle is that: *'If a candidate can't be bothered to make the effort, when they should be trying to make a good impression, then what will they be like when we've employed them? So thank you, but no thank you.'*

As I said earlier, funny as these stories are they are all disaster stories, where someone has missed an opportunity of a job by creating a bad impression, so let's look at how you can create a positive impression.

## How to make a positive impact: body language and dress

When we communicate with people in a face-to-face setting we use two principal ways to transmit our message – words (content and voice tone) and body language.

- The 'word message' is made up of the words spoken and the way the words are spoken.

- The 'body language message' is the message we project through our gestures, actions and the way we dress.

Now, interviews are all about talking, usually one-to-one, with another person, aren't they? You would be forgiven, then, for thinking that when you first meet someone you are going to capture their attention, provided that you have something interesting to talk about! It may surprise you to know that a number of studies have shown that the majority (around 80–90 per cent) of the messages we transmit to other people are through our body language.

We have spent a good deal of time so far in this book concentrating on what should be said in interviews. In this chapter we will look at techniques you can use so that your body language projects the impression that you would want it to project.

## How to use stereotyping to advantage

Whether you like it or not, most people label others within the first few moments of meeting. As much as 90 per cent of a person's impression of you is made in the first four minutes. Some of your initial impact comes from what you say, but the major-

> most people label others within the first few moments of meeting

ity comes from the way you behave and the way you dress – the other person stereotypes you.

To give you an example. In most films what does the 'bad guy' look like? Moustache/unshaven, dark/black clothing and a black hat. He is easy to recognise – Vinnie Jones hasn't played the part of a schoolteacher or parish priest, and as far as I can remember neither has Charles Bronson!

Speak to most rational people and they will argue quite strongly that they 'always keep an open mind when they meet new people' and that they are 'never quick to form an opinion'.

I understand the sentiment. In reality, I'm afraid it's not true.

Try this. Quickly imagine:

| | |
|---|---|
| a secretary | now |
| a plumber | now |
| a school-meals assistant | now |

What was each person wearing? Was the secretary clean-shaven, or did he have a beard or moustache? Was the plumber wearing a dress or a skirt? Was the school-meals assistant wearing a jacket, or was he wearing a sweater? Were you guilty of stereotyping?

You will stand a far better chance of getting the job you want if the image you project, through your dress and body language, creates the right impact – in those vital first four minutes. You need to show that you fit into the stereotype.

Now I know that some people are very uncomfortable with what I have just said, and are probably ready to throw this book in the bin ... 'What about freedom of choice?'... 'No, I'm afraid what they see is what they get'... 'If they don't like me as I am then I'd rather go elsewhere.' If this is the way you feel then fine, I respect your opinions. What I will say, however, is that you are almost certainly shortening your options.

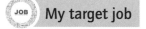

## My target job

What is your stereotype of someone doing your target job? How do they look? How are they dressed? What does their body language say? Make a few notes here.

_____

_____

_____

## How to make a positive impact

It is impossible to generalise and give a definitive 'this is what you should wear for interviews', since all jobs have different requirements. In addition, as organisations evolve 'casual cultures' and flexible working patterns emerge it makes it almost impossible to be definitive.

Imagine yourself in the following clothes: if you are a man you are wearing a dark-blue pinstriped suit, a white cotton shirt with double cuffs, a 'sincere' striped tie, well-polished black lace-up shoes and a plain-faced watch. The female equivalent is the same with no tie, a white cotton blouse and black court shoes.

If you dress like this, your body language is about as persuasive and influential as your dress can let you be (we'll call this No. 5 dress).

Some years ago, studies carried out by IBM found that people dressed as I have just described were 40 per cent more believable than those who were 'less powerfully' dressed.

The less believable end of the scale is the camel-coloured suit, brown shoes and coloured shirt (No. 1 dress). While higher up come the light greys (No. 2 dress), with dark greys even higher (No. 4 dress). Watch the politicians and other public figures on television to assess what effect their dress has on their 'believability quotient' with you. Dark blues or black clothes combined with a white shirt or blouse command authority. It isn't an accident that police and prison officers wear this colour combination, but beware, in the wrong place they may make you look stuffy, unapproachable and too formal. I wouldn't suggest this combination, for example, for an interview for a nursery nurse or a pub landlord.

| | 'Believability' points | Style of dress |
|---|---|---|
| *Increasing believability* | 5 | Dark-blue pinstriped suit, a white cotton shirt with double cuffs, a 'sincere' striped tie, well-polished black lace-up shoes |
| | 4 | Dark-grey or blue suit |
| | 3 | Mid-grey, brown or blue-suit |
| | 2 | Light-grey suit |
| | 1 | Camel-coloured suit, brown shoes and coloured shirt |

Allan Pease is one of the world's leading writers and broadcasters on the subject of body language and stereotyping. His books are good but his films are even better. If you need convincing of the impact of dress on stereotyping, go to YouTube and search for a film entitled *Body Language with Alan Pease* (exact same title); the film is 2hrs 21 minutes long. Alternatively, follow this link: www.

youtube.com/watch?v=Aw36-ByXuMw and scroll forward in the film to 1hour 49minutes and 20 seconds. The film may be a little long in the tooth, but the message is still current and very powerful.

Since the days of the IBM study, things have moved on and I believe it's true to say that many organisations now have a more informal dress code. IBM now even has a 'smart casual' culture, with formal dress being reserved for client meetings. But dress codes vary across organisations: the finance director of one company may wear a dark-blue No. 5 suit while their counterpart in another organisation may go to work in T-shirt, jeans and trainers. There isn't even any consistency across professions: one of my local schools insists on 'business attire' for teachers, and it's written into the teachers' contracts, while another one actively encourages a friendly informal learning environment by asking staff to wear more casual clothes such as chinos and polo shirts, with suits reserved for parents' evenings! Whatever dress code is appropriate to the culture, you can't go wrong if you're neat, clean and well groomed. As a rule of thumb, for your interview you should aim to dress one level higher than the day-to-day work attire. Here are some general principles.

> you can't go wrong if you're neat, clean and well groomed

- Decide where on the 1–5 scale you want to be, so that your dress is appropriate to the job. Lovely as that new suit is (you know, the one you bought for your brother's wedding), ask yourself if it is right for the job interview.

- Clean, well-pressed clothes in good repair – there aren't any buttons missing from the shirt/blouse you're planning to wear are there?

- Wear some perfume or aftershave – but make sure it's not too overpowering. Be subtle.

- If you keep pets, brush your clothes thoroughly – those cat hairs will start to look three feet long if you spot them on your clothes in the middle of an interview!

- Polish your shoes until you can see your face in them – except for suede ones!

- If you're carrying a briefcase, give it a polish.

- For men – earrings and white socks are a turn-off for most recruiters.

- For women – if you're wearing a new skirt, try the sit-down test when you buy it; is it too short? I once interviewed a young woman who sat through the whole process with her top coat on her lap. She'd bought a new skirt for the interview and only realised how short it was when she sat down in it for the first time on the bus, on the way to the interview – too late!

- Beware of silk shirts and blouses – perspiration can really spoil their smart appearance.

- If you wear nail polish use neutral colours.

- If you wear jewellery ask yourself if it is appropriate or too loud.

- Carry a spare pair of stockings/tights in your bag.

- Take only one bag with you into the interview. Fumbling between a handbag and a briefcase can make you look disorganised and reduces your confidence.

- A number of my friends have benefited from 'having their colours done' by taking advice on colours and tones to suit their skin and hair colour. The downside is that it's quite expensive – you may need to change your wardrobe! The positive side is that most of them feel it was beneficial.

If you are leaving education, returning to work after a career break, switching career – such as leaving the armed forces or the police – or making any career step that takes you into a new work culture, it really is worth giving careful thought to the image you want to project. You may need to make a 'transformational' image change to give yourself the best chance.

## Positive impact – body language

Non-verbal communication accounts for about 90 per cent of the message in your interview!

*What* you say is only 10 per cent of the message the interviewer is receiving from you.

In addition to standing tall, smiling and being warm and friendly towards interviewers, the following will help you to send out positive messages.

- Don't wait in reception with your legs stretched out, feet crossed and hands clasped behind your head – you'll look as if you're ready to watch *Match of the Day* rather than attend a formal job interview!

- A handshake: rightly or wrongly, people read all kinds of interpretations into people's handshakes, from the limp lettuce non-assertive to the knuckle-crushing bully! A firm but gentle 'middle ground' handshake is usually appropriate to start and end interviews.

- When you sit down, sit upright but not too stiffly. This shows that you are comfortable and confident. Cowering gives the impression of nervousness and low self-esteem, while a sloppy or relaxed posture suggests a careless attitude and a lack of energy. If you sit on the edge of your chair you can come across as being nervous and tense.

- Don't clutch onto a handbag or briefcase. It will make you look nervous.

- Don't crowd the interviewer's personal space by getting too close; in Western society, 4–6 feet is about as near as you should get to someone in an interview.

- Relax and lean forward a little to give the message that you are interested and involved. If you are leaning back you may appear to be too relaxed and casual, while leaning sideways makes you look uncomfortable.

- If you tilt your head very slightly to one side you'll come across as friendly and open; keeping it straight shows that you are self-assured and authoritative.

- Hold eye contact – but don't stare. When you want to show that you are actively listening, use direct eye contact and maintain it. Avoid looking as if you are staring aggressively by blinking at regular intervals and nodding occasionally. Hold eye contact for about 10 seconds before looking away briefly and then re-establishing eye contact. Beware, as overusing direct eye contact can come across as challenging or dominating to the interviewer.

  Don't look down constantly at the floor – it makes you appear insincere and shows a real lack of confidence.

- Mirror the interviewer's body gestures – if the interviewer crosses their legs, do the same. If they raise their hand to their face, copy their gesture to produce a 'mirror image'. You are telling the interviewer that you are in agreement with their ideas or attitudes. Make sure that your mirroring is natural; otherwise it will look like mimicking! If you want to observe mirroring, go along to your local pub and watch people making each other feel relaxed by mirroring.

- Vary the tone and pitch of your voice; a monotone is boring and you'll sound as if you're not interested in the job, but don't overdo it as you may come across as excitable or emotional.

- Pause and take a breath before answering questions – this gives you time to react in a considered way and makes you look in control.

- Don't sit with your arms crossed – they form a physical block or barrier and send out an 'I don't believe you' message, or make you look defensive. As a general principle, the less you move your arms and hands about the more confident and in control you will appear to be.

- If you don't know what to do with your hands, rest them, loosely clasped, in your lap or on the table. Moving your hands above the neck and fidgeting with your face or your hair is a sign of nervousness. Body language experts suggest that touching your nose or lips can indicate that you are lying, holding one hand behind your head can be a sign that you are annoyed and two hands clasped behind your head can look confident at the right time and domineering on other occasions!

- Keep your emotions on an even keel; smile and nod appropriately, but don't overdo it. Avoid erupting into laughter on your own, but by the same token don't hold a stoic deadpan face!

> speak in a voice that is confident and not apologetic or defensive

In summary, always bear in mind that you are meeting the interviewer as an equal, not a subordinate. Speak in a voice that is confident and not apologetic or defensive, and use appropriate gestures and body language to project a confident positive image.

# How to read the interviewer's body language

You can gauge the interviewer's level of interest in you by observing their body language.

- Pulling or poking their ear – they've heard enough. Move on.

- Hand clenching or clenching the chair arm – they're not impressed with your answer. Change the subject.

- Readjusting their cuff/watch strap – they're bored. Move on.

- Sitting back – they want to listen.

- Leaning back with hands clasped behind the head – they want you to convince them.

- Rubbing the chin suddenly – they're interested in what you're saying.

- Index finger pointing up and resting on the cheek – they're evaluating what you're saying.

- Leaning forward and rubbing hands together – they're very interested in what you're saying.

- Regularly looking at their watch – they are bored with your answers or conscious that the interview is over-running. Keep your answers brief and to the point.

# Last impressions

A last impression from me!

Don't get so 'hung up' about gestures, actions and dress that you forget about the content of the interview! Watch people in real life or on television for examples of what I'm talking about.

When you attend an interview, a few well-chosen gestures and nicely matched attire will help you to create that perfect impression in the first four minutes.

# Chapter 11

## How to give a great presentation

To assess your self-confidence, ability to communicate and ability to handle a mini-project, some organisations may ask you to make a short presentation, either to a group of managers or, for very senior positions, to the board of directors. Others incorporate a presentation into their assessment centre exercises.

The subject can vary – debating the pros and cons of such topics as e-commerce or mobile communications, or you may be asked to present a mini-marketing plan for one of the company's products. They may even leave the choice of subject to you. If this happens do not pick 'Where I took my holiday' or 'My hobby'. Do choose a business-related subject that you know something about. The time you are given to prepare can vary from 30 minutes to many days.

If you are asked to give a presentation do take it seriously – management time is very valuable and if the company has gathered an audience to listen to you, then you can be sure that they will be taking it seriously.

Unless you are a natural, or are very experienced, you will probably be nervous. This is a good thing. If you don't have at least some degree of anxiety then you probably aren't taking the exercise seriously. There isn't a magical cure for presentation nerves, but you CAN overcome and control your nerves by preparing your presentation as thoroughly and professionally as possible and by practising your presentation, ideally in front of an audience.

> the keys to an effective presentation are preparation, planning and practice

The keys to an effective presentation are preparation, planning and practice.

## Prepare the content

Most people find knowing where to begin is the most difficult step. If you are one of these people I can guarantee the following steps will help you present confidently. *Please*, for the moment, resist any temptation to switch on your PC! That comes later.

Ask yourself – 'What do I want the audience to learn from my presentation?' Write this objective in the middle of a blank page. Now let your mind 'freewheel' to produce a mind map of ideas. The mind map included here below is the one I drew when I started to plan this chapter, which was originally published as an article called 'How to give a presentation and live to tell the tale'.

You'll find that you have far too many things to say, so the next step is to edit and give the presentation some structure. Choose the most important point you want to communicate. Write it on the presentation planner (see page 214) as key point no. 1. Now add the others in descending order of priority.

Yes, I know that the natural tendency is to save the best to last, but remember that people are most attentive at the start.

Now develop your content by putting the information from your mind map into your key points. Remember, only information that is relevant to achieving your objectives is allowed. Limit your key points to a maximum of five – three is even better. Think about presenters you admire – are they those who put over a powerful and succinct argument or are they those who waffle and constantly overrun?

You have now developed the main body of your presentation. But before we move on, decide how you will bridge from one point to the next. A phrase such as, 'Now let us look at the introduction' lets the listeners know you've finished one topic and gives a signpost to what's next.

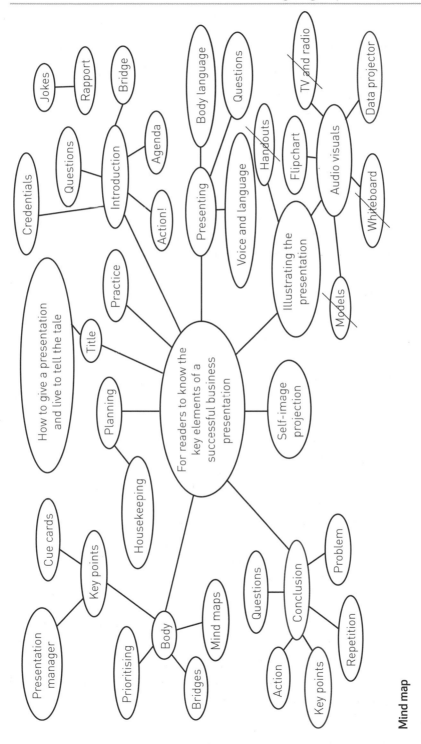

**Mind map**

Other useful bridges are:

- Enumerating – 'first ..., second ..., etc.' – when you've stated that you have a specific number of points to cover.

- 'On the contrary' or 'On the other hand' when you're weighing pros and cons, or simply 'Next ...'

- To avoid sounding hackneyed, use a different bridge to move from each of your key points.

Now write them on your presentation planner.

## Your introduction

You get one opportunity to make a first impression. So how do you create that positive impression from the start?

The first step is to establish empathy by building a bridge to as many audience members as you can. If possible, speak informally to each person before you begin.

When you stand to address the group, reinforce the bridge by saying how much you've been looking forward to meeting them ... and pay some compliment to their office, factory, etc.

If you're considering starting with a joke, my advice is don't. You never know who you may offend and alienate. This isn't to say you shouldn't be warm, friendly and charming. But, as well as having the potential to offend, comedy is the most difficult of all stage techniques to master, as any actor will tell you.

Now say what you're going to talk about, as seen from their viewpoint. Why should they listen to you? You should say a few words here about why you are qualified to speak on this topic, what you have done to research the subject, what your background is in this field, etc. Two or three sentences can establish your credibility.

Now for the agenda. Give the audience a 'map' of what you'll be talking about. The agenda is a list of the key points that make up the body of the presentation. 'As we go through the presentation, please feel free to ask questions if I haven't explained anything clearly – although there will be a few moments at the end for questions.' Let's face it, telling people to save their questions until the end rarely works. So why not prepare for it? Doing it this way also signals to the audience that you're confident of what you're talking about.

Next, state quite clearly what you want them to do as a result of listening to you – the action request. 'When I've finished speaking I hope you will see that the strategy I am advocating will help to re-position (product) in the marketplace.'

And finally your bridge. How do you link to the first key point in the body?

Now write each of these into your presentation planner.

## The conclusion

Your conclusion should be short and to the point, but not rushed. You want to encapsulate your presentation into a package that they can take away with them.

Remind them of the problem or opportunity. Restate your key points and crystallise the message. State your request action – what you want them to do.

This structure for your presentation ensures that your key points are repeated at least three times and repetition is a very powerful persuader. Just watch commercial television to see how often advertisements are repeated if you need convincing.

Now write your conclusion on your presentation planner, shown below.

To summarise (with apologies to whoever said it first) your structure will allow you to 'Tell them what you're going to tell them, then tell them, and then tell them what you've told them.'

## Presentation planner

| Introduction | Main body | Conclusion |
|---|---|---|
| Rapport statement | Key point 1 | Remind them of the problem/opportunity |
| Presentation subject | Bridge | |
| Your credentials | Key point 2 | Restate the key points and crystallise the message |
| Agenda | Bridge | |
| Question request | Key point 3 | |
| | Bridge | |
| Action request | Key point 4 | Request action |
| | Bridge | |
| Bridge | Key point 5 | |
| | Bridge | |

## Plan your resources

Now you have decided what you are going to say, you can concentrate on how you say it. Transfer your introduction, key points (in the correct order) and conclusion on to postcards, using single words to act as stab points. Do not write a script, it will make your voice become dull and lifeless.

Now punch a hole in the top right-hand corner of each card and loosely tie them together with a piece of string. This will keep your presentation in the correct order, even if you drop the cards. When you deliver your presentation, don't be afraid to glance at your cue cards. A momentary pause is far more acceptable than waffle or a deathly hush because you can't think what to say next.

Visual aids are useful in your presentation since they can convey information – try describing in words the layout of a printed circuit board or how to fold a napkin! Your visual aids reinforce what you are saying by focusing the audience's attention.

The most convenient visual aids to use are flipcharts or whiteboards. Or, if you're a high-tech expert, interactive whiteboards.

The flipchart can be very useful for developing diagrams in front of your audience – write the words/draw the diagram in advance lightly in pencil on the flip-chart sheet. The audience will not be able to see the fine lines and you will be confident that the layout will be correct when you start to build up the chart in front of your audience using marker pens. Ensure that you have at least two pens available and check that they both work before the presentation.

Nowadays you'll be out of the running if you don't use one of the software packages such as PowerPoint. You may even be asked to take your presentation visuals on a memory stick or CD, so that they can be projected using an electronic data projector. PowerPoint has become the standard for producing presentations, so here are some tips.

## Making your point with PowerPoint

If you've never used PowerPoint to create a presentation, ask around among your friends for some help. PowerPoint is a tremendous tool in helping to create powerful presentations. With a few clicks of a mouse you can bring a car, a caribou or even Concorde into the room!

However, we've all heard the expression 'death by PowerPoint'. Too many people confuse the medium with the message, and use all the whistles and bells of PowerPoint to create boring repetitive screen shows or confusing circus acts, with fade-ins and fade-outs and all the other trickery!

Here are my top tips for getting the best out of PowerPoint.

- Use a consistent slide design with an uncluttered background for all your pages. Create a master page (Menu Bar/View/Master/Slide Master) and the layout will then be consistent for all the new pages you create.

- Use a consistent colour palette – don't start to fiddle around with the colours that are recommended in the font or text palette – they are there because they complement each other and don't clash. However, if you can match the colour palette to the company's corporate branding then you send a subliminal message that 'you're already one of the team'.

- Avoid sending your audience to sleep by using page after page of bullet points and subheadings – words on a screen are not visual aids! Use short stab points like you see on a billboard. One main heading and then a maximum of four bullets points is plenty. Don't put your script on the screen. If you remember the rules of 4by5 and 33 you won't go too far wrong: maximum of 4 lines of 5 words each, and no more than 33 words on any slide.

- Use visuals whenever you can. BUT avoid using the Microsoft clipart or sound files that came with your PC – they will have seen it all before. Use your scanner, your digital camera, a clipart library from your computer store or trawl the internet. For example, if you right click on the company's logo on their website, you can save it to 'My pictures' and then use it in your presentation as an image in the footer of the master slide, so that it's there on every slide. Animations can also be used as very powerful images, but don't overdo it. Animations are available free at: **www.animationlibrary.com**.

- Include diagrams and flow charts – a picture is worth a thousand words! Better still, a 10- to 15-second clip of video – but if you know how to add clips of video you probably don't need these tips! Short clips of video can be downloaded from websites such as YouTube, using free software packages such as YouTube downloader (use Google to find the link). If you do insert music or video files remember that you'll need a sound system that is loud enough for the audience to hear, so check beforehand that the presentation room has the appropriate facilities. Also remember that the video or music clip links to a file on the hard drive of the computer where the presentation was created. So if you have to copy your presentation onto a different computer you'll have to make sure the music/video files are also copied onto the other computer and that you have re-established the links. In a similar way, provided you know you're going to have reliable internet access you can use embedded hyperlinks so that you can link directly to a remote website during your presentation. If these techniques are new to you and you decide to use them, make sure you have had a play and have practised beforehand and that you're thoroughly confident in your abilities to control them, and not the other way round. It may sound complicated but it isn't, and it can make the difference between a boring, routine, 'sausage-machine' PowerPoint show and a job-winning presentation!

- When you've created the presentation, ask yourself 'What can I edit out and still keep the meaning?' Be ruthless when editing – cut out everything that is not absolutely necessary. Work on the basis of about one slide for every minute of your presentation.

- Use only one font throughout, or two if you need a specific contrast. If you want to emphasise a word, use font size, bold, italic or colour, but don't underline.

- When people look at a new slide, their eyes will move from the top-left to the bottom-right of the screen. Artists quote the two-thirds/one-third rule for creating balance in a picture. In a nutshell, put your visual 'bottom-right' – two-thirds down and one-third from the right.

- If you use transitions, use the same simple one throughout until you want to highlight a change of subject or really emphasise a point.

- Remember that each slide is part of a process. So, when you've finished preparing, run the slideshow to make sure that the sequence flows comfortably and fits in with the 'story' that you developed using the Presentation Planner.

- Finally, if you know you have to use someone else's computer or laptop, make sure you find out which version of PowerPoint they are running and save your presentation as the correct version. Why? Software packages are usually backward compatible, but may not be forward compatible. If you create something in PowerPoint 2003 it will probably run fine in compatibility mode in PowerPoint 2010. You may not be so lucky if it's the other way round, and you don't want to find that out as you are about to face your interviewers!

Remember, if you emphasise *everything*, you emphasise nothing. KISS – keep it sweet and simple. On the logistical side of things, do what you can to make sure that you will be able to read your file in the software on their PC when you come to present it. If you've got the latest version of the software and they have an older version there may be problems. Why not save a couple of versions to CD/ DVD just to be sure? When I give talks at conferences I usually e-mail a copy to the organiser, take a copy on a portable hard drive and also take my laptop with a copy on the hard drive. You might think I'm a bit obsessive/neurotic, but I've never had a problem. Unlike one friend of mine who picked up his ultra-slim notebook by the corner and cracked the hard drive just before a presentation. Or another friend who tried to be clever by using an obscure font in his slides – unfortunately the font wasn't installed on the PC at the conference centre. They both 'busked' their way through, but I guess it's not really what you'd want to do at a job interview! It doesn't look professional, and it doesn't show you at your best.

Whichever visual aids you use, follow the basic principle of keeping them as simple as possible. Use large letters and single words as stab points so that they can be read easily. Do not write complete sentences. Remember, a picture is worth a thousand words. As a general rule, allow about one minute per slide when planning your time.

## Practise

Rehearse your presentation once or twice so that you know what you are going to say and how you are going to say it. Use a friend as a timekeeper and to give you constructive feedback.

## Answering questions

Generally speaking, assessors are aware of your time pressures and so will save their questions until the end. If you're asked a question that you can't answer then be honest – you'll gain more credibility from this than from half-baked waffle. You can, in fact, turn your lack of knowledge to your advantage by answering: 'That's an interesting point that I haven't been asked before. I'm afraid I don't have an answer for you right now but I will find out and get back to you.' This technique flatters the questioner's ego and demonstrates your integrity.

## Preparation and presentation

Get a good night's sleep and, no matter how nervous you are, avoid alcohol or stimulants!

Here are a few dos and don'ts for you to bear in mind when presenting.

| Do | Don't |
| --- | --- |
| Use global vision to include everyone | Use non-words, such as ums and errs |
| Hold eye contact with people | Jingle coins/keys in your pockets |
| Check the power situation beforehand | Scratch or twitch or fiddle with your hair |
| Check the focus of the projector beforehand | Talk to the floor, screen or just one person |
| Set up the room beforehand | Read visuals word for word |
| Use clear, concise visuals | Joke – you don't know who you might offend |
| Vary the tone and speed of your voice | Mumble |
| Stand relatively still | Apologise for what you're going to say |
| Have spare pens/transparencies | Dress outrageously |
| Keep to time | Use a pointer – they're too easy to play with |
| Use simple language | Remove your jacket |
| End on a positive note | Overrun! Stick to your allocated time |

## What are the assessors looking for?

Unless you've applied for a job as a television presenter, or a similar position that involves speaking to groups on a regular basis, it is unlikely that the assessors will be looking for outstanding skills.

The assessors will be looking for you to communicate your message effectively, for you to project yourself confidently and for you to know what you are talking about. They'll also be trying to gauge how much work you have put into the exercise and how seriously you took it. I once ran an assessment centre in which two of the candidates were 'late entries'. Each received the briefing pack only the day before. One candidate gave a very poor talk from some scribbled notes and apologised, making the excuse that she hadn't had time to prepare. The other candidate gave an excellent presentation, with professionally produced transparencies and handouts of her talk for the assessors. She made no mention of the short amount of time she'd had to prepare. Let me ask, who do you think made the best impression? And, everything else being equal, who would you have employed?

Finally, remember that even the most experienced presenters get nervous – use the adrenalin to help you to excel!

remember that even the most experienced presenters get nervous

Below is an example of a marking sheet that the interviewers may use to assess your presentation.

# Assessment Centre – Presentation Score Sheet

Candidate name: _____          Assessor: _____

Ten-minute presentation with five minutes of questions and answers from assessors.

| Criteria | Comments | Rating |
|---|---|---|
| Content | | |
| Delivery (voice/posture) | | |
| Pace | | |
| Use of visuals | | |
| Audience contact | | |
| Handling questions | | |
| Other comments | | |

### Standards

5   Much more than acceptable (significantly above criteria required for successful job performance)

4   More than acceptable (generally exceeds criteria relative to quality and quantity of behaviour required)

3   Acceptable (meets criteria relative to quality and quantity of behaviour required)

2   Less than acceptable (generally does not meet criteria relative to quality and quantity of behaviour required)

1   Much less than acceptable (significantly below criteria required for successful job performance)

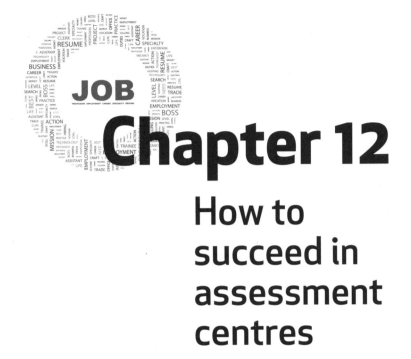

# Chapter 12

# How to succeed in assessment centres

Assessment centres were first pioneered in the UK by the armed forces and are now used by a number of organisations to select people for jobs. They are very often called 'development centres' when used for internal selection purposes, or to identify fast-trackers and people with potential for promotion. For most candidates it's a once-in-a lifetime opportunity. Depending on the job, procedures can last from half a day to three days or more.

In the early part of my career I (successfully!) attended a couple of assessment centres as a candidate, and since my move into HR management I have run dozens of assessment centres. So I hope the following 'inside information' will be useful. See also the chapters on presentation skills, interview skills and tests and evaluations. The table at the very end of this chapter summarises the exercises at a typical assessment centre and shows how candidates are assessed.

## What will happen?

The event will usually be run by a chairperson/facilitator. They will mastermind the whole day and will probably welcome everyone in a group and say goodbye at the end. They will also run a series of group exercises and tests. They'll also be observing the way everyone works together and be gathering an overview of the 'group dynamics'.

Then there are the observers. They will have been trained and briefed before the meeting. Each observer will be allocated a person or people to observe and they will take copious notes and 'mark' the performance of the candidates. Halfway through the day, observers may 'switch candidates' so that a better-balanced view is obtained.

So how can you outshine the other candidates, and demonstrate that you're the 'best match' for the job?

- Get as much sleep as you can in the days beforehand and try to arrive refreshed. Assessment centres will burn up your adrenalin reserves ... and more! It's highly likely that, just as you're starting to relax, you'll be handed a mammoth task with a tight deadline to see how you respond under pressure.

- Keep your eyes and ears open and observe the performance of the other candidates. You may be asked to rate their performance. Be prepared to give a factual and analytical summary of their contribution. Don't be afraid of criticising other candidates and don't be afraid of praising them – but make sure it's based on facts. Sometimes you will be given a piece of paper at the end and asked to rank all the candidates (including yourself).

- If you've been invited to join everyone the night before the assessment centre, don't be lulled into a false sense of security by thinking the assessors are off-duty. They will probably be assessing your social competence over dinner, in the bar, over breakfast ...

- Even if you haven't been asked to prepare a presentation, brush up on your skills. There is a good chance that you'll be asked to prepare one at short notice. Pre-select two topics – an 'improvement you've made at work' and an 'interesting angle on your hobby'.

- If you're invited to attend an assessment centre in a hotel, a few casual questions to the manager or receptionist may give you a good idea of what's in store. If the assessors have spent the early part of the day setting up a network of computers in syndicate rooms, then it sounds as if you're going to be involved in a computer-based business simulation. Great fun!

- Try to think through the qualities the assessors will be looking for – leadership, interpersonal skills, ability to handle stress, verbal communication, written communication, flexibility, negotiation skills, problem solving, business skills, commercial acumen, decision taking, initiative and creativity. Clearly the weightings will change depending on the job, but commercial acumen, interpersonal communication skills and flexibility must be high on everyone's list.

- Don't try to suppress other candidates in an attempt to make the assessors notice only you. You will come across as overbearing and insensitive.

After the assessment centre finishes for you, then the real work of the chairperson and observers begins! The chairperson will now lead a process to evaluate each against the performance standards that were set beforehand. The objective is to try to make the selection process as scientific and as objective as possible. I can tell you from personal experience that these meetings can last a long time, and even into the early hours of the morning!

## Assessment centre exercises

Assessment centres are usually designed to include exercises that will measure you against the aspects of the job. **For all of the exercises, make sure you understand the chairperson's instructions or the written brief. If you don't understand, ask!**

Not listening and not reading instructions thoroughly are the two biggest causes of frustration in candidates. I have been moaned at, and even shouted at, by candidates who had not read instructions properly. Losing your temper and having a go at the chairperson is a career-limiting step, I can tell you! And it does happen – I once sent a candidate home from an assessment centre at lunchtime after she'd lost her temper twice! What a waste of an opportunity. Remember, you're being tested!

The following are common exercises.

## In-box/in-tray exercises

These can be paper-based or electronically based. You are given the 'in-tray' or 'in-box' of a senior manager and have one hour to 'get through it' – otherwise you'll miss your plane! You'll be asked to make notes of what you will do with each item, or write a reply to letters, phone messages or e-mails.

- *Quickly* sort the whole pile first and prioritise every item – A (top priority), B and C. They have probably 'buried' some important items, like a resignation of a member of staff, near the bottom!

- Start with the As and work your way through.

- Resignations and other 'people' issues are top-priority As.

- Wherever you can, make a note that you would make a telephone call, or send an e-mail – the MD of one of my client companies says that he writes no more than four memos per year.

- If you do write memos, write key messages and let your 'secretary' compose the letter. Familiarise yourself with the organisational structure and the briefing instructions before you start, so that you know who's who.

You can find a free practice in-tray exercise at: **www.assessment day.co.uk/in-tray-exercise.htm**.

You can also find a free practice e-tray at the Civil Service Fast Stream selection site: **faststream.civilservice.gov.uk/How-do-I-apply/Example-e-Tray-Excercise** (*sic*).

## Sales or negotiation role play

You are asked to sell a product or negotiate a deal.

- Ask 'probing' questions – how?, why?, when?, where?, what? and which? are best for gathering information.

- Listen to the answers and try to match the needs of the customer with what the product does. To give an example, one of the all-time favourites when recruiting new salespeople is for the interviewer to say, 'OK sell this fountain pen to me'. Unenlightened candidates immediately start prattling on about style, design, gold nibs and good ink flow. The smart ones ask questions such as, 'Do you use a fountain pen?', 'What qualities arc important to you when you're choosing a new pen?', 'What would you expect to pay for a fountain pen?'. They then go on to match the product's features and benefits to customer needs.

People who do badly in these exercises do so because they're too busy putting over their own viewpoint, based on assumptions, rather than asking questions to find out what the 'customer' wants!

## Business simulation

This may be paper-based or computer-based. You are split into small groups and, over a series of rounds, compete to develop, manufacture, market and distribute products. Great fun!

- Play to win!

- Invest in research for new products in the early rounds – products don't last for ever.

- As you get results back at the end of each round, analyse the performance of the competitors – you may be able to undercut them or market your product to a niche audience.

## Group discussion (interactive skills)

You are given a problem to solve as a group. Common problems are simulations where your group has been stranded at sea, in the desert or on the moon. (See the end of this chapter for an example of an assessor's form.)

If you're 'stranded' in the desert or on the ocean, being detected is the first priority, followed by food; don't move away to try to save yourself – search parties look for your last location! Try to work out which items you have that can be used as signalling devices.

- Formulate your own ideas quickly and sell them convincingly to the group.

- Suggest that the group needs a structure and timetable to work to – and propose one.

- Don't steamroller other people's ideas, listen attentively.

- If someone isn't contributing, draw them into the group by asking for their ideas.

- Five minutes before the end suggest that you need to summarise your decision and take control, or suggest that someone takes control, of whatever needs to be done.

There are many other types of exercise. For example, if you're applying for a commission in the forces or for other leadership roles, you'll almost certainly be given a series of 'command task' exercises where each person takes a turn at acting as leader. If this is likely to happen, do some reading on leadership skills in advance – I'd recommend *The One Minute Manager* and also *Leadership and the One Minute Manager*, both by Dr Ken Blanchard (whose co-authors were Spencer Johnson on the first and Patricia Zigarmi and Drea Zigarmi on the second). If you're applying for a job in marketing you may be asked to write a marketing plan showing how you would launch a new product, or relaunch a failing product. If you're applying for a line management job you might be given an overview (hypothetical or real) of the team you'll be taking over and the management issues you'll be faced with, and asked to give a short presentation on how you would handle them.

## Make the most of your opportunity

You'll find an excellent resource for preparing for assessment centres at the Prospects website. Although primarily intended for recent graduates, the advice is applicable to most candidates: www.prospects.ac.uk/interview_tests.htm.

An assessment centre is a tremendous opportunity for you to show what you can do. Prepare yourself well and enjoy it. In summary, be positive, be prepared to play the game and project an image of your real self.

# INTERACTIVE SKILLS ASSESSMENT

Candidate name: _____          Assessor: _____

| Behaviour | Quality/quantity of contribution | Rating |
|---|---|---|
| Giving information | | |
| Seeking information | | |
| Supporting others | | |
| Disagreeing with others | | |
| Persuading others | | |
| Controlling others | | |
| Other contributions | | |

**Comments**

**Standards**

5   Much more than acceptable (significantly above criteria required for successful job performance)

4   More than acceptable (generally exceeds criteria relative to quality and quantity of behaviour required)

3   Acceptable (meets criteria relative to quality and quantity of behaviour required)

2   Less than acceptable (generally does not meet criteria relative to quality and quantity of behaviour required)

1   Much less than acceptable (significantly below criteria required for successful job performance)

**Overall rating** _____

**Selection Panel Assessment Form: Position** _____

Chairperson: _____        Interview date: _____

Other panel members: _____

## EXERCISE

| Candidate | Leaderless group | In-tray exercise | Presentation | Marketing plan | 1:1 negotiation | Interpersonal/ social skills | Interview no. 1 | Interview no. 2 | Assessment |
|---|---|---|---|---|---|---|---|---|---|
|  |  |  |  |  |  |  |  |  |  |
|  |  |  |  |  |  |  |  |  |  |
|  |  |  |  |  |  |  |  |  |  |
|  |  |  |  |  |  |  |  |  |  |
|  |  |  |  |  |  |  |  |  |  |
|  |  |  |  |  |  |  |  |  |  |

Panel recommendation: _____

# Chapter 13

## How to win in recruitment tests and evaluations

### Personality, skill and aptitude evaluations

Some organisations use tests and evaluations in their selection process. Before inviting people to interview, the recruiter identifies personality traits, skills and knowledge that the ideal candidate would have. During the selection process candidates are asked to complete 'tests' to evaluate whether they possess these qualities.

The extent of the testing can vary from a short five-minute form-filling exercise through to a whole day, involving a battery of tests and evaluations and an interview with a psychologist.

I cannot stress too strongly that there is no need to get anxious about the tests! I know it's easy for me to say that ... I'm not the one who has been invited to the interview! Seriously, the tests will not reveal that really you are an alien from Mars (you aren't, are you?) and just for today you've transformed yourself into a person! Take them in your stride, do your best and be honest in your replies. One of the major objectives of the evaluations is to find square pegs for square holes; if you 'cheat' by giving replies that you think will get you the job you may be lucky and get a job, but you may also find that you're a round peg in a square hole and the job's not right for you. Worse still, six months later you may be back on the job market!

> there is no need to get anxious about the tests

## Personality questionnaires

As the name implies, these questionnaires aim to gain an insight into your personality. I do not like the use of the word 'test' when related to personality evaluations. 'Test' implies 'right or wrong', and in personality evaluations there are no right and wrong answers – we are all different.

Usually no time limit is set for completing a personality questionnaire, but you are advised not to over-analyse your replies and to move quickly from question to question. Don't answer questions as you think you *should*. Be honest with yourself, otherwise you're defeating the object. Also, some personality questionnaires have an in-built evaluation that checks to see how consistent (honest) your answers have been.

> be honest with yourself, otherwise you're defeating the object

The most commonly used personality questionnaires are:

- Myers-Briggs Type Inventory (MBTI), which claims to be the most widely used in the world: **www.myersbriggs.org/**.
- SHL Occupational Personality Quotient (SHL OPQ): **www.shldirect. com/personality_questionnaire_examples.html**.
- OPP's Sixteen Personality Factors (16PF): **www.opp.eu.com**.
- PPA (Personality Profile Analysis) Thomas International: **www.thomasinternational.netourassessments.aspx**.

There are many others.

## Skill and aptitude tests

Unlike personality questionnaires, skill and aptitude tests are designed to test you against standards. Typing tests are used to evaluate your keyboard skills and typing accuracy. Tests of manual dexterity, such as rebuilding a broken-down model, assess your 'motor skills'.

Others represent an intellectual challenge: numerical, verbal and abstract reasoning tests. The score from the tests is compared against 'norm' tables to see how you have performed, compared with previous groups of people who have taken the test.

If you're going to be asked to take a test it will be on a PC or on-line and possibly before you are invited for interview.

Fortunately some self-assessment testing organisations offer their services on-line to help you evaluate your own skills, interests and values so that you can focus your career goals better. Even better, many employers have practice tests on-line, so that you can self-evaluate whether you are right for the job or simply overcome your nerves.

Google 'Recruitment Tests' or 'Practice Recruitment Tests' and you'll find lots of examples (beware some of them make a charge) or, alternatively, have a look at the following websites:

| | |
|---|---|
| Army | www.army.mod.uk/join/20289.aspx |
| Assessment Day | www.assessmentday.co.uk |
| Practice Aptitude | www.practiceaptitudetests.com |
| SHL | www.shldirect.com/practice_tests.html |

In addition, many university careers websites have links to practice tests, e.g.:

| | |
|---|---|
| The University of Kent | **www.kent.ac.uk/careers/psychotests.htm**. |

## 'Team type' questionnaires

Work by Dr Meredith Belbin has shown that groups are most productive when there is a good mixture of people who can contribute various skills to the team. The organisation will analyse the members of the existing team. The 'team type' questionnaire is then used and your results are analysed manually or by software to see how you fit in.

None of the team types is the 'best' type to be – productive teams have a mix of the different types. The following summary describes the various team types.

- **Plant** – creative, imaginative, unorthodox. Solves difficult problems. Weak in communicating with and managing ordinary people.

- **Resource investigator** – extrovert, enthusiastic, communicative. Explores opportunities. Develops contacts. Loses interest once initial enthusiasm has passed.

- **Chairperson/coordinator** – mature, confident and trusting. A good chairperson clarifies goals, promotes decision making. Not necessarily the most clever or creative member of a group.

- **Shaper** – dynamic, outgoing, highly strung. Challenges, pressurises, finds ways round obstacles. Prone to provocation and short-lived bursts of temper.

- **Monitor evaluator** – sober, strategic and discerning. Sees all options. Judges accurately. Lacks drive and ability to inspire others.

- **Teamworker** – social, mild, perceptive and accommodating. Listens, builds, averts friction. Indecisive in crunch situations.

- **Company worker/implementer** – disciplined, reliable, conservative and efficient. Turns ideas into practical actions. Somewhat inflexible, slow to respond to new possibilities.

- **Completer** – painstaking, conscientious, anxious. Searches out errors and omissions. Delivers on time. Inclined to worry unduly. Reluctant to delegate.

- **Expert/specialist** – single-minded, self-starting, dedicated. Provides knowledge or technical skills in rare supply. Contributes only on a narrow front.

To find out your own 'team type' I would strongly recommend Meredith Belbin's book, *Management Teams: Why They Succeed or Fail*, which contains the questionnaire and also a free voucher to take an on-line evaluation. You can also get useful information from www.belbin.com. Learning about your team type can be advantageous because it tells you about your strengths and also tells you which team roles you should avoid.

## Drug and alcohol testing

Because of their concern about the effect that alcohol and drug abuse has on productivity, some employers may require you to provide a urine sample that will be tested for drugs and alcohol. These tests are still quite rare in the UK but are common in the USA, so they are probably more likely to be encountered if you are applying to the UK affiliate of a large US company. Of course you can always refuse – but if you do so then you'll almost certainly eliminate yourself. I'm not here to debate the pros and cons, but common sense would suggest that if it's likely that you'll be tested and you're likely to test positive, then give yourself a clear period to 'detoxify' before the interview or medical check!

## Graphology (handwriting analysis)

You won't even be aware that this evaluation is being carried out! Graphologists claim to be able to interpret the personality of a person from their handwriting. I understand that it is widely used in continental Europe, particularly in France and Germany, but not in the UK – although one UK consultancy offering this service has over 100 clients.

If you want to read more about drug and alcohol testing or graphology visit the website of the Chartered Institute of Personnel and Development, and use their search engine at www.cipd.co.uk.

## Use and interpretation of tests

An employer will be using ability measures and personality questionnaires to find out broadly how someone will cope with the particular intellectual demands of a job on the one hand, and how they will conduct themselves in approaching tasks, interacting with others and perhaps dealing with pressure on the other. In order to make these interpretations, your performance will usually be compared with that of a 'norm group' of others.

Those working with tests and personality questionnaires should abide by the professional standards laid down by the British Psychological Society and the Institute of Personnel and Development. Among other things, these say that feedback should be given to those tested. If this is not forthcoming when you are tested, ask about it! For personality measures, feedback is often used as part of a further discussion with you as the candidate. This is partly to check that the measure is giving a realistic picture of you. It is also to provide further information to expand the indications from the questionnaire. To use the example of orderliness, if you appear to score high on this you may be asked to give evidence of situations where you have demonstrated this and where it has been particularly important in the past.

Sometimes ability tests will be used as part of a screening process, and sometimes to provide additional information on a group of candidates all of whom have been shortlisted. In the screening case a definite cut-off score is likely to be applied. Where tests and questionnaires are used at the shortlist stage they may often result in a detailed report. This will be considered by a final selection panel, along with other information such as that taken from a CV or from a presentation to the panel. Professional use of tests also requires that they should never be used as the sole determinant of whether or not someone is offered a job but should be set in the context of such other information.

## Preparing for testing

The advice given for exams of 'get a good night's sleep' applies to testing. It is also a good idea to allow yourself plenty of time to arrive at the testing location and, as far as possible, to clear your mind of other matters. If you are waiting for the test to finish so that you can dash out and check for messages on your mobile phone, you are unlikely to be giving the test your best shot!

## Feedback

To end on a positive note, many employers will give you feedback from these tests, whether you get offered the job or not – but usually only if you ask!

Profiling instruments, evaluations, assessments, or whatever you wish to call them, are not free – they cost the recruiting organisation both time and money. If they're being used, they're serious about your application.

They are yet another way for you to show you're the right person for the job!

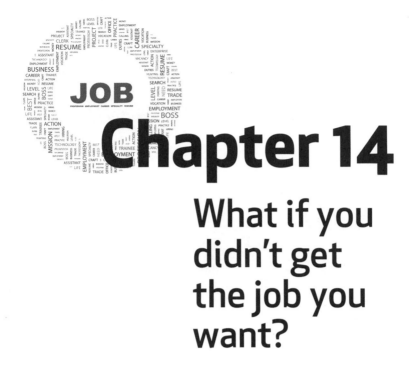

# Chapter 14

## What if you didn't get the job you want?

You made it to a shortlist of two. People were making such positive noises about how you would fit into the organisation. And then a letter this morning: 'Thank you for attending interview ... I am sorry to inform you that ...' and the world falls away from under your feet.

## Can you turn the situation to your advantage?

There can be very few of us who 'enjoy' rejection, if any, and I'm not going to patronise you by making facile remarks such as 'remember tomorrow's another day ...' But once you have got over the disappointment it may be worth seeing what you can learn from the experience.

- Write to them quickly to say how disappointed you are not to have been chosen and how impressed you had been with their company. Say that if any other vacancies arise in the near future you would like to be considered.

- Alternatively, telephone them to say the same things and to ask for some feedback on why you didn't get the job – most employers will give you some constructive critique and, you never know, you may be able to re-open discussions – it can work. A friend of mine who is a partner in an accountancy firm once offered a job to someone who did just this. After the 'regret' letter went out a new opening came up and the employer had planned to start the recruitment process all over again; a perfect example of a win/win situation

- Follow up your letter or e-mail with a phone call.

- Some employers have a policy of not giving feedback; remember they have no obligation to do so. So, if they ignore your calls or don't respond to your letter don't take it personally!

- What have you learned from the process? It may be not to put all your eggs in one basket or to conduct yourself differently at recruitment interviews.

## How NOT to handle rejection

This is a response to a rejection for a job with a drinks company, which was supplied by their personnel manager, who commented: 'I wonder what we didn't see in him?'

*I received your rejection of my application today. Thanks for nothing! I will have you know that in psychometric tests carried out by two leading recruitment consultants I was found to be in the top 10% of graduates both times. I regularly score century breaks at snooker, I am a highly rated footballer and can bench press 120kg. I am also extremely good looking. With a CV as good as mine, for you not to even offer me an interview borders on the scandalous. Who are you after for this position, Superman?? However, being this brilliant I have to accept there are incompetent people in every area of life, including recruitment. Anyway, I accept your rejection with extreme contempt and wish you every misfortune for the future.*

One of the other advantages of telephoning for feedback is that it can give you 'closure' so that you can move on to the next applications. You may also realise that the job might not have been the best use of your skills. It may be a bitter pill to swallow at the time, but probably best for both parties in the long run. A natural reaction may be to think negatively about your performance in the interview, but the feedback might be that the employer was very impressed with you, but you were just beaten to the winning post by someone who was a better match. It may also give you an opportunity to develop your skills. To end this chapter on an even more positive note, here's a wonderful true story of a candidate who 'snatched victory from the jaws of defeat'.

## JOB How learning from feedback can bring success

This true story was kindly supplied to me by a fellow member of the Chartered Institute of Personnel and Development:

*I once gave feedback to an unsuccessful candidate for an admin role. She hadn't come close to being appointed, so I was able to give her plenty of constructive hints and tips on how she could improve her interview technique. A few months later, a similar role came up in the same office; the lady applied again, was interviewed by the same managers and got the job! Her interview performance had improved considerably to the point where she beat a strong field.*

*So I guess the moral of that story is: ask for feedback and if you get it, think about it and act on it.*

Jacqueline C, an HR manager

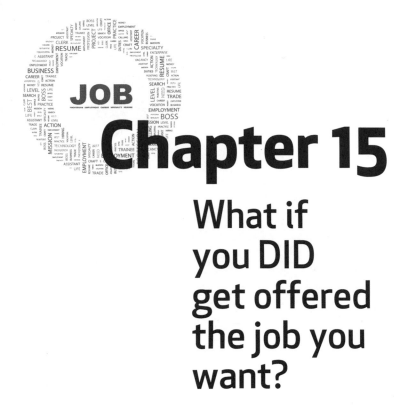

# Chapter 15

## What if you DID get offered the job you want?

Congratulate yourself! CELEBRATE!

And don't forget to say thank you to those who helped you on your way.

'Yippee, I got the new job!' (candidate's view). 'Yippee, I've filled the vacancy!' (employer's view). It's what's called a win/win scenario by negotiators. Both parties have benefited.

As soon as your potential employer starts to display buying signals you should be ready to begin the negotiation concerning your earnings package.

I've said earlier that you should let the employer raise the issue of salary first, but you should also realise that they may not necessarily make their best offer up-front.

## Negotiating the best package

*'What we obtain too cheap, we esteem too lightly; it is dearness only that gives everything its value.'*

Thomas Paine

In some occupations, salaries are fixed according to seniority and length of service. In others there is a good deal of flexibility around certain variables. Remember, when you have accepted an offer, you have accepted it. You'll create a bad impression if you accept the job and then go back two days later, trying to renegotiate the terms of the contract. So before you enter the negotiating arena it's worth working out the minimum package you are prepared to accept and what you would like to get. Realistically, there will be some aspects of the package that will be fixed, for example holidays, and will be written in policies and procedure, but other aspects may be negotiable. The information on salary surveys in the next section should be useful in helping you to negotiate a better deal.

## Salary surveys – knowledge is power

Salary surveys are produced by agencies that gather (confidential) information from many organisations on the salaries paid to people at all levels (but names are never released). This information is 'pooled' and analysed, and then shared between the contributing organisations. HR managers can then look at the tables to see how their organisation's salaries compare with others, and use the data when preparing job offers. Salary surveys can be specific to a particular industry or profession, or they can be based geographically.

Some organisations, which 'want to recruit the best', have a philosophy of paying at the 'ninetieth percentile' – they pay better than 90 per cent of their competitors. Others pay at the median – halfway up the scale. But remember that for every high payer there's another at the bottom of the scale!

There can be large differences between the minimum and maximum salaries and 'benefits', like values of company cars. In one salary survey that I looked at, the lowest paid job pays £17,000 a year with no company car, while the highest pays almost £32,000 with a £15,000 company car. A huge difference, yet these people hold the same job title but in different organisations. If everything else was equal, which job would you prefer? If you Google 'salary surveys' you'll find dozens of websites that can help you to get a good indication of what you are worth in the marketplace. Also some of the recruitment websites, including **totaljobs.com**, have a salary checker that can give you the going rate for your job and any alternatives: **www.totaljobs.com/salary-checker/salary-calculator**.

While you are in the discussion phase of negotiation, before anything is committed to paper, ask:

- Where does the salary fit into their internal salary scales?

- Where does the salary fit in the salary surveys, for a person with similar experience doing a similar job?

Company policy may be that they pay a 'lower quartile' salary (in other words, 75 per cent of people doing a similar job earn more) to a new starter, with the objective of shifting you to the upper quartile within three years. Try to convince them that your skills and experience warrant being started higher up the scale.

Don't be greedy, but do be thorough. Many of the employment agency websites contain salary calculators and advice. Also remember that you probably won't be able to renegotiate a package once you have accepted it so tread carefully. An extra £500 per year over a career is an awful lot of money! And it does work. I was once offered a lecturing post at the base starting salary. I returned the contract with a polite letter to HR pointing out that the offer did not seem to take into consideration my previous years of experience and while I hadn't expected to be placed on the top of the scale, I had hoped for the mid-point. Less than a week later I received a new offer letter and contract at the mid-point. If you don't ask, you don't get! *QED*.

> if you don't ask, you don't get

## Departing diplomatically from your current job

*'Don't flatter yourself that friendship authorises you to say disagreeable things to your intimates. The nearer you come into relation with a person, the more necessary do tact and courtesy become.'*

Oliver Wendell Holmes

### The personal aspects of leaving your current job

If you are leaving on bad terms, DON'T, DON'T, DON'T be rude, abusive or disrespectful to your ex-employer. No matter how much venom there is on the inside, control it and keep it there.

Now, I'm not offering this advice in the interests of your ex-employer, but in yours. No matter how bitter you are feeling, try to leave on amicable terms. The reason for this is that most new employers will want a reference from your past employer. Even if you don't need it immediately for a new job, you might need it in a year or two. You'll do neither your self-esteem nor your future job prospects any good if you lose your temper and are abusive to your boss.

> no matter how bitter you are feeling, try to leave on amicable terms

If you want to vent your anger, try writing a letter to your ex-boss. Don't hold anything back. When you've finished, and said everything you want to say, tear it up and throw it in the waste bin! It does work!!! (And if you've written it on a PC make sure it hasn't been saved!) Perhaps you should avoid doing this at work, just in case!

Try to 'negotiate' the wording of your reference before you leave so that it can be placed on your personnel file. People move on and it may be that, even only a few months after you have left an organisation, a personnel officer you have never met will complete a company reference for you and this will be based on the contents of your personnel file.

You can find tips and templates for writing your letter of resignation at **www.i-resign.com.**

## The practical aspects of leaving your current job

Ensure that you erase any personal information that you may have stored in your user area and, also, if your user area contains information that will be needed by other people, make sure you pass on any passwords.

If you are responsible for holding any company equipment, particularly if you work from home, ensure that it gets returned to the appropriate person. You don't want to accidentally forget to return the data projector that you stored in the loft, only to find six months later that your ex-colleagues remember you as '*the guy who nicked the data projector!*'

Organising your pension might not seem all that important at present as you make plans to start your new job, but as retirement approaches you'll want to be sure that you made the correct decision. Make sure you know the name of the pension fund administrator so that you can keep them updated of changes of address and also whether you want to change pension schemes/ transfer funds into another scheme.

In a nutshell, do everything you can to leave on a professional note, so that your now 'ex-employer' will continue to say good things about you in the future.

# Starting your new job: the new kid on the block

*'Ah, but a man's reach should exceed his grasp, or what's heaven for?'*

Robert Browning

Congratulations! What you have reached for has come within your grasp! Everything we have been working on together has come to fruition. If I can offer some final advice, don't hide this book away in a cupboard and forget about it – come back to it now and again to see how well you are progressing against your goals. And don't forget what we have been saying all along about transferable skills. In your job hunt you have been developing a wide variety of transferable skills – active listening, interpersonal communication and networking to name just three. Transfer them with you into your new job – don't leave them in the cupboard.

You get only one opportunity to create a first impression. So here are a few things to think about. I hope they will help you to take the right first steps on your new journey.

- Find your way around: you'll probably get a quick tour of your workplace, either by your boss or a colleague, during your first day so that you can get to know where the essential places are – refreshment areas, stationery cupboard, fax, photocopier, etc. If this doesn't happen, ask your boss or a colleague to show you in your lunch break. The sooner you know your way around, the sooner you'll feel at home.

- You can choose a lot of things in life but, just as you can't choose your family, you can't choose your boss! Work on building a good relationship. Identify his/her working style and standards. Find out what's important to them.

- Get to know the rules; what might have been taken for granted at your previous job may be entirely different in the new one. Find out about lunch breaks – when you can go, how long you have, etc. Tread carefully and ask. Don't abuse your e-mail or the phone for personal use. Only give your work e-mail address and phone number to friends when you have established that it's OK.

- Create the right first impression, whether through punctuality, dress or the quality of your work – you're being watched and labels are applied very quickly and last for a long time. I was nicknamed 'Smiler' (ah well, could have been worse) at the age of 11 and am still known by that name to some of my friends! And 'do unto others ...' – it's what I call the difference between personal power and positional power. People who rely on positional power expect others to click their heels and come running, just because they're the group chief accountant or because they're a supervisor. People with personal power get things done because of their respect for others and their ability to treat them decently.

- Set the standards. If you're unhappy with the quality of people's work then address it quickly and tactfully. If you're pleased with people's work then say so. Everyone likes praise!

- Work hard at fitting in. Make a determined effort to learn everyone's names. Write them down or get hold of a staff list, so you can see who's who: it's usually on the shared drive. Get to know your colleagues. Ask them a bit about themselves; what do they do, how long have they worked here? Accept invitations to join people for a coffee or for lunch (even if you like to be alone at break times, make an effort to join others if you're invited). Similarly, accept an invitation for a drink after work if you can; it's a strong sign of acceptance that you are being seen as part of the team. In spite of your efforts, there's a good chance that there will be someone who doesn't 'see you as their cup of tea', or you may have similar feelings towards them. That's life isn't it? Just do your best to act professionally in your dealings with them.

- Identify and make friends with your Taffy and John. Taffy was the head of security and John was the maintenance man at the last company I worked at. They had a finger on the pulse of everything that was going on in the building and could sort anything from a broken-down car to a hotel booking. I swear that if I'd needed to charter a 747, one of them would have been able to arrange it, and if they couldn't they would have known a 'man who can'! And while you're about it, what about making sure you introduce yourself to the IT technician, and your HR officer and … The quicker you build working relationships with colleagues, the quicker you'll fit in and the more you'll enjoy your new job.

- Read your job description and understand what's expected of you. If you haven't got one, ask for one – or better still, offer to write it!

- Ask your boss for feedback – 'How am I doing?'

- If you don't have an induction programme, ask for one. If there isn't one, then design it yourself so that in the first month you'll make contact with everyone you'll interact with during the course of your work. Which do you think is better for building productive relationships, sitting in an ivory tower and exchanging e-mails with someone you have never met or telephoning, say the production manager, and asking 'I'm new to this industry, could someone show me the production line so that I can see exactly how we make our products?'

- Don't be a shirker. Accept new challenges with enthusiasm. Clock-watchers, 9–5ers and those who shy away from work have a short 'shelf life'.

- Don't keep going on about how wonderful things were at your last company. By all means bring in new ideas, but don't become a CD stuck in replay mode.

- If you're going to make changes, think through how you're going to communicate the changes, how you're going to implement them and what the impact on others will be. How will you handle their reaction? Transformational changes (we were travelling north, we did a handbrake turn and now we're going south west!) tend to ruffle more feathers than incremental changes (if we turn the wheel gently then ...). There's a place for both kinds of change, but for both think it through, then follow through.

- Say thank you; people love to be appreciated. If people have been helpful to you, why not thank them by taking in a bag of doughnuts or a box of chocolates for coffee break on Friday morning at the end of your first week. Less than a fiver's worth of doughnuts will buy you a fortune's worth of goodwill!

Good luck in your new job.

I wish you every success.

*When you win ... nothing hurts.*

Joe Nameth, New York Jets

# Thank you

This book would never have become a reality without the help, support and advice of a great number of people. I am especially grateful to the thousands of career and life planners and job hunters who have bought the previous editions. Knowing how useful the information and exercises have been to them was the inspiration to write my first book and has sustained me through many long hours at my desk as I have written each new edition.

I have made every effort to make the text of this book non-discriminatory. If I have failed in any part, please accept my apologies and let me know, so that I can correct it for future editions.

## Share these lessons with others

Malcolm Hornby frequently speaks, throughout the UK, on all the aspects of job hunting and career and life planning covered in his books. If you would like to invite him to speak at your conference, seminar or meeting please write to him c/o Professional Division, Pearson Education, Edinburgh Gate, Harlow, Essex CM20 2JE, or e-mail: Malcolm@Hornby.org.

Visit the website of this book at: www.Get-That-Job.co.uk.

# Appendix 1

## Sources of help for job hunters

The internet is not static, and as some websites close down another ten open to take their place! If any of these links becomes inactive please let me know, so that we can correct things for the next edition, by e-mailing me at Malcolm@Hornby.org.

If you have a suggestion for inclusion in the directory, please let me know at the same e-mail address. Inclusion in this directory does not constitute an endorsement, either by the author or the publisher. You'll find these links and more at my website: www. get-that-job.co.uk.

### Legal and general advice

ACAS: www.acas.org.uk

Citizen's Advice: www.citizensadvice.org.uk

Employment law: www.emplaw.co.uk

Equality and Human Rights Commission:
www.equalityhumanrights.com

Trades Union Congress website – choose 'Work rights':
www.tuc.org.uk

The Tribunals Service: www.employmenttribunals.gov.uk

## Rehabilitation of offenders

Law on the web: www.lawontheweb.co.uk/rehabact

NACRO: www.nacro.org.uk

## Disability

Royal Association for Disability and Rehabilitation:
www.radar.org.uk

## Recruitment websites

These are my top five recruitment websites, based on user-friendliness, useful information and number of jobs.

1  Reed: www.reed.co.uk
2  Totaljobs: www.totaljobs.co.uk
3  Monster: www.monster.co.uk
4  Jobsite: www.jobsite.co.uk
5  Fish4jobs: www.fish4.co.uk/iad/jobs

The government also has an excellent website, Jobcentre Plus:
jobseekers.direct.gov.uk

## National newspapers

*Daily Express*: www.express.co.uk

*Daily Mail*: www.dailymail.co.uk

*Daily Mirror*: www.mirror.co.uk

*The Daily Telegraph*: www.telegraph.co.uk

*Financial Times*: www.ft.com

*The Guardian*: www.guardian.co.uk

*The Independent*: www.independent.co.uk

*Mail on Sunday*: www.mailonsunday.co.uk

*The Observer*: www.observer.co.uk

*Sunday Mirror*: www.sundaymirror.co.uk

*The Sunday Times*: www.thesundaytimes.co.uk

*The Times*: www.thetimes.co.uk

## Professional journals/newspapers

Admin/secretarial: www.Londoncareers.net

Architectural: www.arplus.com

Automotive: www.motortrader.com

Entertainment and stage: www.thestage.co.uk

Hospitality: www.caterer.com

Legal: www.lawgazette.co.uk

Legal: www.thelawyer.com

Marketing: www.mad.co.uk

Media: www.nma.co.uk

Medicine: www.thelancet.com

New media: www.marketingmagazine.co.uk/go/revolution

Nursing: www.nursing-standard.co.uk

Online recruitment: www.onrec.com

Personnel/HR: www.personneltoday.com

Public finance: www.publicfinance.co.uk

Public relations: www.prweek.com

Scientific: www.nature.com

Scientific: www.newscientistjobs.com

Teaching: www.tes.co.uk

## Training providers and advice: learning and skills development

Learndirect: www.learndirect.co.uk

Open University: www3.open.ac.uk/courses

Vision2learn: www.vision2learn.co.uk

## Researching companies

Kompass 2.2 million companies: www.kompass.com

## Career and life planning

Personality evaluation. Take the Kiersey Temperament Sorter at: keirsey.com

Portfolio working. Take the self-test to see whether you could become a portfolio worker at: www.creativekeys.net/portfoliocareertest.htm

Work–life balance. Design your 'ideal' life pie.
For a Microsoft Excel tool to help you to do this, visit: www.eoslifework.co.uk/getalife.xls

## Skills and aptitude tests

| | |
|---|---|
| Army: | www.army.mod.uk/join/20289.aspx |
| Assessment Day: | www.assessmentday.co.uk |
| Practice Aptitude: | www.practiceaptitudetests.com |
| SHL: | www.shldirect.com/practice_tests.html |

In addition, many university careers websites have links to practice tests, e.g.:

The University of Kent: **www.kent.ac.uk/careers/psychotests.htm**

## Salary checker

Totaljobs.com:    **www.totaljobs.com/salary-checker/ salary-calculator**

# Appendix 2

Don't take 'No' for an answer – perseverance pays! There's a saying (modified from the Bible): *'The race is not given to the swift nor the strong but those who endure until the end.'* As I said earlier in the book, you'll only succeed in your job hunt by persevering in spite of the nos! To keep you on track here's an inspiring A–Z (well almost!) of stories of people who have overcome failure, ridicule and rejection and achieved success. I do hope that their examples will inspire you to keep going to the end and achieve success in your job hunt.

**Astaire, Fred:** The casting director of MGM famously observed that Astaire 'Can't act. Can't sing. Slightly bald. Not handsome. Can dance a little.' Astaire went on to become an incredibly successful actor, singer and dancer and kept that note in his Beverly Hills home to remind him of his roots.

**Beatles, The:** In early 1962, four young Liverpool musicians travelled down to London to audition for Decca Records. They were rejected by Decca who said 'We don't like their sound, and guitar music is on the way out.' The group, who happened to be called The Beatles, became the biggest band in the world, selling over half a billion records within ten years.

**Beethoven, Ludwig van:** A German composer of classical music, Beethoven is widely regarded as one of history's greatest composers. But at the start of his career, Beethoven's music teacher once said of him 'as a composer, he is hopeless'.

**Chaplin, Charlie:** The iconic funny man of the silent movie era, and successful producer and director, was initially rejected by Hollywood studio chiefs because they felt his character/act was a little too nonsensical to ever sell.

**Churchill, Winston:** In a poll conducted by the BBC in 2002 to identify the '100 Greatest Britons', participants voted Churchill as the most important of all. Yet Churchill struggled in school and was regarded as an academic failure. After school he faced many years of political failures, as he was defeated in every election for public office until he finally became Prime Minister at the age of 62.

**Darwin, Charles:** The founder of the theory of evolution and an outstanding scientist was often chastised by his father for being lazy and too dreamy. Darwin himself wrote, 'I was considered by all my masters and my father, a very ordinary boy, rather below the common standard of intellect.'

**Disney, Walt:** The Disney organisation generates billions of dollars from merchandise, movies and theme parks around the world, but Walt Disney, the founder, had many personal failures before he achieved success. After being fired by a newspaper editor because, 'he lacked imagination and had no good ideas', Disney started a number of businesses that ended in bankruptcy and failure. He kept trying and learning, however, and eventually found a recipe for success that worked. The Walt Disney Company now makes an average revenue of US $30 billion annually.

**Edison, Thomas:** His teachers told Edison that he was 'too stupid to learn anything'. When he started work things didn't improve and he was fired from his first two jobs for not being productive enough. As an inventor, Edison made 1,000 unsuccessful attempts at inventing the light bulb. One day, an assistant asked him why he didn't give up. After all, he had failed over a thousand times. Edison replied that he had not failed once. He had discovered over 1,000 things that didn't work. What a positive mental attitude!

**Einstein, Albert**: One of the leading scientists of the twentieth century, Einstein was awarded the 1921 Nobel Prize for Physics. For most of us, Einstein's name is synonymous with genius, but it was not always the case. Einstein did not speak until he was four and could not read until he was seven, causing his teachers and parents to think he was mentally handicapped, slow and anti-social. Eventually, he was expelled from school and was refused admittance to the Zurich Polytechnic School. He may have been a 'slow starter', but I think most of us would agree that he did a good job of catching up!

**Ford, Harrison**: In his first film, Harrison Ford was told by the movie executives that he simply didn't have what it takes to be a star. This didn't deter the young actor who, in 1997, was ranked No. 1 in Empire's 'The Top 100 Movie Stars of All Time' list, and who at about the same time was the highest earning actor in the world!

**Goddard, Robert**: Goddard today is hailed for his research and experimentation with liquid-fuelled rockets, but during his life-time his ideas were often rejected and mocked by his scientific peers who thought they were outrageous and impossible. Today rockets and space travel are part of our everyday life, due largely in part to the work of this scientist who worked against the feelings of the time.

**Grey, Zane**: Incredibly popular in the early twentieth century, this adventure-book writer began his career as a dentist, some-thing he quickly began to hate. So, he began to write, only to receive rejection after rejection for his works, being told eventu-ally that he had no business being a writer and should give up. It took him years, but at 40 Zane finally got his first work pub-lished. He now has almost 90 books to his name and has sold over 50 million copies worldwide.

**Grisham, John**: This best-selling novelist's first novel was rejected by 16 agents and 12 publishers. He went on writing and writing until he became best known as a novelist and author for his works of modern legal drama. The media has coined him as one of the best novel authors of the twenty-first century.

**Honda, Soichiro:** The founder of the Honda Corporation was turned down by Toyota Motors when he applied for a job as an engineer after World War Two. He was equally unsuccessful when he applied elsewhere and instead started to make home-made scooters, which he sold to his neighbours. Subsequently, he started his own company. Today, the company has grown to become the world's largest motorcycle manufacturer and one of the most profitable car manufacturers.

**King, Stephen:** King's iconic thriller *Carrie* was rejected 30 times, finally causing him to give up and throw it in the bin. His wife fished it out and encouraged him to resubmit it, and the rest is history. King now has had hundreds of books published and is one of the best-selling authors of all time.

**Lincoln, Abraham:** Regarded by many as one of the greatest leaders of the United States of America, in his early life it didn't appear as if Lincoln was destined for success! He went to war a captain and returned a private. He started numerous businesses that failed, and went bankrupt twice. He was defeated in 26 elections before his political career finally took off and subsequently he was elected the 16th President of the United States of America.

**Monet, Claude:** Monet's iconic impressionist paintings now sell for millions of pounds and hang in some of the most prestigious galleries in the world. Yet his work was mocked and rejected by the artistic elite, the Paris Salon, because it 'bucked the trend' of the existing Renaissance style. Undeterred, Monet ignored the experts and continued his impressionist style, which influenced others to 'set a new trend' that continues to be popular more than a century later.

**Monroe, Marilyn:** In 1947, one year into her contract, she was fired by 20th Century-Fox because her producer thought she was unattractive and couldn't act. That didn't deter the young Ms Monroe at all and she kept on going and eventually achieved fame and success. Indeed, she is regarded by some as the twentieth century's most famous film star, sex symbol and pop icon.

**Morita, Akio:** Along with his partners, Akio founded Sony, but one of their first products, an electric rice cooker, was a disaster and they only sold 100 cookers because it burned rice rather than cooking it! Today, Sony now ranks as one of the world's largest electronic and electrical companies.

**Newton, Isaac:** Newton didn't do well at school and failed miserably when he was put in charge of running the family farm. An uncle took charge and sent him off to Cambridge. The failed farmer went on to become one of the greatest scientists the world has even known!

**Poitier, Sidney:** After his first audition, Poitier was told by the casting director, 'Why don't you stop wasting people's time and go out and become a dishwasher or something?' Poitier vowed to show him that he could make it, going on to win an Oscar and become one of the most well-regarded actors in the business.

**Sanders, Harland David:** Better known as Colonel Sanders of KFC (the worldwide chicken restaurant franchise), Sanders had his famous secret chicken recipe rejected 1,009 times before a restaurant finally accepted it.

**Schultz, Charles:** The 'Peanuts' comic strip is one of the best know in the world, but its creator, Charles Schultz, had every cartoon he submitted rejected by his high school yearbook and was rejected for a job working with Walt Disney as a cartoonist.

**Spielberg, Steven:** The American film director has won three Academy Awards and ranks among the most successful filmmakers in history. He was recognised as the financially most successful motion picture director of all time. During his childhood, Spielberg dropped out of school. He was persuaded to return and was placed in a learning-disabled class. His return lasted only one month after which he dropped out of school forever. Although today Spielberg's name is synonymous with big-budget blockbuster films, he was rejected from the University of Southern California School of Theatre, Film and Television three times.

**Van Gogh, Vincent:** A failed artist? During his lifetime, Van Gogh sold only one painting, and that was to a friend for a very small amount of money. He persevered, sometimes going without food so that he could complete his over-800 known works. Today, his paintings sell for millions!

**Wayne, John:** Before his successful acting career, in which he played numerous tough heroes, he was rejected as unfit for the United States Naval Academy because of an old football injury.

**Winfrey, Oprah:** Oprah Winfrey is one of the richest and most successful women in the world, but she travelled a hard road to get to that position. She had a rough and often abusive childhood, as well as numerous career setbacks including being fired from her job as a television reporter because she was 'unfit for television'.

**Woolworth, Frank Winfield:** Woolworth was once one of the biggest names in department stores. Before starting his own business, however, young Woolworth worked at a store but was not allowed to serve customers because his boss said he lacked the sense needed to do so. Woolworth also had many ideas of how to market products – all of which were rejected by his boss. His ideas became the foundation of his phenomenal retail success with his own stores.

---

**Don't take 'No' for an answer – perseverance pays!**

# Index